In The Beginning...

GEMS FROM GENESIS

ASTOUNDING GEMS OF TRUTH
IN GENESIS SURFACED *ENROUTE*
ON PILGRIMAGE

LUCILLE L. TURFREY

Paperback: 978-1-960861-17-7
eBook: 978-1-960861-18-4
Library of Congress Control Number: 2023907756

This is a work of nonfiction.

..... oOo .....

In The Beginning began early one morning as I was just awakening and contemplating the happenings of the day ahead. The concept was there, quite suddenly, so much so that I felt as though pushed from my bed to go at once to the computer room. It was early December. The final full stop was placed on the 1st draft on 31 December—a good way to conclude the year with thanksgiving in my heart!

The riches of these *Gems from Genesis* are deeply embedded in my mind through many years as a teacher of truths pertaining to Scripture—in Australia, Scotland, and Russia. These truths are embedded in my soul through the deepening of my personal faith through the years. All content—including photography, art, poetry, and paraphrasing of Scripture—is by the author. Where I have drawn upon my poems previously published by The Salvation Army, Australia, such are used by permission, and noted by an * preceding titles. I am deeply indebted to Mavis Smith, my brilliant proof-reader who has, yet once again, tackled the pages with her trusted "tool". Thanks, Mavis, you are a *"Faithful"* friend.

An occasional soliloquy, pages 36-37, 82-83, 118-119, 134-135, 154-155, drawn from my major work, *Shadows and the Light*—a poetic Companion to the Bible (Revised Edition)—are included, having the intent of adding texture to the Biblical records relating to the predominant "gems" of Genesis: the main characters. The author holds copyright to that book, also published by Sweetspire Literature.

The photographs throughout this book are selected as "Picture Parables" to introduce each gem and its Biblical theme.

CONTENTS

CONTENTS

..... oOo .....

In The Beginning ...

THE SPARK

A spark!
That's all it took,
A sabred shaft of light
That lit the night;
The empty void was pierced!
The universal orbs,
Excited into resonance,
Once burst upon the sullen night
And galaxies were formed
With purpose evident:
To dance their course in light!

A spark!
That's all it takes,
A sacred shaft of light
To light the mind
And pierce a vacant space;
The human soul is powered.
Awakened into vibrancy,
The spirit is infused with "light"
And brings to life a plan,
A purpose evident:
To walk with God in light!

LLT

PREFACE

As a tourist, I have been blessed by the grandeur of nature's offerings in distant lands. I have walked the soils of many climes, with vistas brought up close by trekking in the well-defined tracks of intrepid travellers, past and present.

My tourist jaunts among many cultures have also enriched my understanding of how nature reclads herself after the winter's somnolence. I am blessed by how springtime's blossom spells hope, summer's leafy-green canopies display confidence, and autumn's golden foliage shouts thankfulness. The mountains have challenged me, the valleys gladdened me, the wilderness amazed me, the metropolis emboldened me. Such are the blessings found in the "top soil" of life.

Surprisingly, I have been caused to consider that there is as great a range of colour under the surface-soil as that above! The opal says it best. But look at the ruby, the jasper, the topaz, the emerald, the sapphire, and the amethyst. Here is the "rainbow" not dependant upon sunshine on the rain!

Deeper observations have caused a change of outlook, of in-look! The tourist has become a pilgrim! What is the difference? I have already given a wide-ranging description of the tourist in me. My tourist life was "respite" life as I allowed nature to "renew" my body and mind... But wait, what of my soul? In choosing to change my altitude of thought to that of the pilgrim, my travelling days are now of a different ilk! There is purpose in my stride, I hold an aim—a goal—to attain.

The pilgrim is one who has not only a changed viewpoint in the journey but there has been a change in purpose. The pilgrim sets out on a sacred journey towards a desired goal. Tourists need their maps and guide books to keep on track. Just so, the pilgrim cannot do without the selected Guide Book. This pilgrim has selected the Bible! *In The Beginning* will discourage travellers from skimming the surface, traversing along the top-soil without pausing in their stride in order to make use of a proverbial "spade" when intent on discovering the riches that do

Preface

abound under the surface of the alluvial soil of experience. The gems that gleam beneath the surface will enrich the soul!

The aim of back-tracking to "The Beginning" is to bring a greater clarity to the textual material provided in Genesis. This book sets out to offer Genesis jewels to the investigator weary of superficial meanderings. Genesis cannot be fully understood until a "spade" is employed to clear away the "surface soil"! I am no miner! Yet here I am, inviting you to dig below the surface of the past, deeper than the superficial discoveries made by chance on the tourist trail. So, come with me, take up your "spade". Join me in this enterprise.

The treasure to be found in the Bible is enriching beyond measure. Its gems are truly astounding, as you will discover from its first viewpoint, the location of which goes by the name of Genesis—genesis being the means of marking the origin of something! In seeking out the gems in Genesis, we will be digging below the surface of the chapters of this, the first book that has placed on record the beginning of all things. But here is the obstacle: HOW AUTHENTIC IS THIS BOOK?

Have we not outgrown the archaic language of the past and its outmoded thought patterns? These questions call for some "spade-work" to be applied to that which we thought we knew, that which may have provided a clearly defined route for the intrepid travellers of the past. The dramatic discoveries made by adept scientists of recent years has prompted many to put that book on a forgotten shelf. What have we lost?

The "spades" residing in my library have their own particular titles and usefulness. Bible translations, Bible dictionaries, commentaries, lexicons, scientific records, for example, have all been invaluable throughout this pilgrimage.

Let us put aside preconceived notions which do not take into account what the original language—Hebrew—is actually conveying, and begin excavation. The Hebrew alphabet—page 158—is provided as a map to assist us as we begin "the dig":

HIDDEN TREASURE: *IN THE BEGINNING*

The sun will always rise at dawn. Light will always overcome night.

A WORD FROM THE WORD

בראשית

barashith - "In the beginning…"

The **tourist** in me will introduce each subject pictorially, and from personal experience, before pondering a viewpoint, then donning the shoes of the **pilgrim** to delve into Genesis. With the first word—*word: the articulation of thought*—God begins the revelation of His being, of His glory and grace: rich treasure!

A VIEWPOINT TO PONDER
What existed before "The Beginning"?

There was no time or space. The Scriptures, however, declare that *from everlasting to everlasting*, God IS! The Dwelling Place of God is Eternity. An eternity which holds a commencing date is no eternity at all! Eternity is eternal! In recorded history, there are instances of people who have, near death, experienced another "existence". Sir Basil Spence spoke of "finding" his design for the Coventry Cathedral during his near-death experience and, after returning to health again, Spence utilised that special design to reconstruct the magnificent cathedral.

PILGRIM'S JOURNAL: Genesis 1:1

The treasure contained between the covers of the Bible is measureless. Hidden beneath the surface of the printed word are gems with which those who would mine, as for gold, will enrich their lives both for time and eternity! Take your "spade", lift the soil. The very first turning of the earth will disclose abundantly more than what one simple word may convey from the "surface" of the page.

Here, at Genesis 1:1, the first word discloses more than the surface of the initial statement. One word? Actually, this is a conglomerate word, as the English translation reveals. Three words in one: *In the beginning*...

The beginning? How long was the beginning? No one knows! Modern science has been able to decipher much from the "encyclopaedia of the rock face". New discoveries continue to hold us spell-bound as to the length of days, seasons, years, ages, eons, that enabled the universe—the Earth in fact—to settle into its rightful place. One thing is for certain: it all happened before "The First Day" according to the Bible records!

Take from the soil this gleaming topaz gem: the time-line tells us nothing more than *In the beginning*... Time as we know it had yet to begin. A closer observation of the Hebrew word makes the matter plain: what God did *in the beginning* was the first, the initial action of creation and it was before *the first day*!

Here, where we stand, was part of "The beginning". What is that description? Oh yes, "third rock from the sun". We were safely set within the Solar System and, while we could not have stood on the soil of Earth on that first day, what a wonder to discover what really happened *in the beginning*!

It is hard to conceive of an everlasting "night" of nothingness! Before *the beginning* there was nought but deep darkness shrouding the face of the deep, a formless void, non-entity, a waste of nothingness, a lifeless, sterile space, infinity of dark, an emptiness enfolded in deep ebony. Yet here was space where God would act to bring about *the beginning*...

HIDDEN TREASURE: *CREATION*

As a mist lifts, the clear view emerges and nature displays her glory.

A WORD FROM THE WORD

בָּרָא
bara - "create"

It is of lasting joy to have hiked the heather-clad highlands of Scotland. The morning mists will cling to the crags until the gentle rays of the sun encourage them to disappear. There is fortitude to be won through discarding the mist, thinking: 'I can do this, I can trek this mountain', then activating the challenge.

A VIEWPOINT TO PONDER
How is it possible to think new thoughts, to clear the fog?

A thought engendered by *inspiration* comes to mind. And, the question must be asked: what is the meaning of *inspire*, utilised so often by the composer, the poet, author, architect, artist, and teacher? But can they be termed "creators"? To be inspired means to think new thoughts, to be energised to actualise a new idea, to undertake a great enterprise that gives rise to an accomplishment beyond one's normal scope of endeavour. It is to be *inbreathed*, empowered, by the Spirit of God to hear and to DO what He implants within the mind and, the soul.

PILGRIM'S JOURNAL: Genesis 1:1

One of the strangest of all Hebraic phenomena can be mined from the first and second words occurring in the Scripture. Before picking up the spade, it should be pointed out that the flow of Hebrew in this first sentence falls uneasily upon the ears of English-speaking readers. This is as follows: *In the beginning created God the heavens and the Earth*—heavens here referring to the skies above the Earth. We must clear the fog.

There is still, in this post-modern world of ours, much ado about whether the thought of **creation** could ever be held as a viable description of what really happened *in the beginning.* Why, it just happened—with a Big Bang!

This unique word, *bara*, is extremely rare. It most certainly is not to be found inserted within the data relating to most of the "days" as outlined in Genesis 1. *Bara* is mentioned only at the strategic times of actual creation—once at the first creation, once at the second creation and three times at the third creation, marking the importance of that third creation.

This may be quite a surprise to many who are familiar with the textual "soil". So, the spade will need to dig a little deeper. But here is the gem: what does the word actually mean? A sculptor can "form" something entirely new from the clay in his hands. But unless he is able to utilise material never before in existence, he does not *create* his masterpiece!

What, then, are the three creations—that which is formed without any extant material—from the Hands of the Creator? Know the true meaning of *create* and the answer comes to view:

1: 1	**MATTER**	the heavens and the Earth
1:21	**MIND**	living creatures (***create***-ures)
1:27	**MEANING**	soul: humans (likeness to God)

In every other aspect of the formation of the universe, the materials were already in existence. With the creation of life, God could now complete what He had contemplated before *the beginning.* It was in the Mind of God to create a being with whom He could communicate–humankind–before TIME began!

HIDDEN TREASURE: *GOD*

Nature's "palette of paint" is the picture of perfection.

A WORD FROM THE WORD

אלהים

elohim - "God"

Having walked in this field, I can ask how a field of yellow, red, and blue tulips should be selected to bring a visual description of God to the page (if that were at all possible)! There is indeed good reason, for the Hebrew word for God is plural: *Elohim.*

A VIEWPOINT TO PONDER
What's in a name?

A name is chosen for many reasons: it's pleasant, it marks an aspiration, it gives honour. My names honour the visiting aunts. The juxtaposition of my two names gives undue emphasis to the meaning of each: First name: *light*; second: *night.* I can live with that. In fact, I find the inevitable *twilight* quite humorous.

The singular form of God's Name in Genesis is *El* though the plural form, *Elohim,* is most frequently used in the Old Testament. Two Hebrew letters mark the difference: ים = *im.*

Elohim—plural? Can **God** be plural? Must we be faced with a plethora of the gods once worshipped before idols, rightly, were cast aside? Such is far from the truth! How, then, can God be considered plural—even if the *im* confirms His plurality?

From ancient times, the people of Israel have remembered these words for they are embedded in the spiritual foundations: *Hear O Israel, the LORD your God is One.* Deut. 6:4.

We must, therefore, come back to the basic question: how can God who is "ONE" possibly possess a Name that is unequivocally plural? Strangely, there is strong evidence that confirms the rightness of the Name for here is God speaking: *Let US make humans in OUR image, in OUR likeness.* Gen. 1:26.

How is it possible, in the realms of reality, that humanity can in any way be a replica of the Divine Being, the Creator of the universe, the Being we are pleased to call God?

We are creatures, but creatures possessing body, mind, and soul. Is not this a TRINITY OF BEING??? We may certainly think of God in terms of The Trinity for we are aware of God the Father, God the Son, and God the Holy Spirit, undivided in essence and co-equal in power and glory.

As a little aside, a field of tulips may well help us to grasp, from the scene, that which is beyond normal comprehension:

> **BLUE**: God: the HOLY Father, utter purity
> **RED**: Jesus: SAVIOUR by His shed blood
> **YELLOW**: The Spirit: Fire, energising POWER.

From the very beginning, the triune "man" (both male and female), is created to be like God! What's more, this most remarkable statement should put us in our correct place–there is no difference in the status of man or woman: we are all ONE!

God is colour-blind and has been so since the creation of the being meant to be like Him! God finds colour, culture, class, and creed as ONE in His Sight, Mind, and Heart. One day we may see from the eyes He gifted us, see as He sees ALL= ONE!

HIDDEN TREASURE: *THE HOLY SPIRIT*

A mother nurturing her brood will engender discipline, ensuring family order.

A WORD FROM THE WORD

רוח

ruach – "Spirit"

It is the second sentence in The Bible that introduces us to the *ruach*, the Holy Spirit. Some early indications should be given here regarding the Hebrew text. First, capital letters are omitted as they were not employed by the ancient writers. Of greater import is the fact that Hebrew is all but devoid of vowels and the omission is regulated, predominantly, by dots and dashes. My transliteration may suffice when Hebrew vowels are absent.

A VIEWPOINT TO PONDER
Did not The Holy Spirit come to Earth at Pentecost?

The *ruach*, The Holy Spirit—God through all Eternity—is introduced in Genesis 1:2. This is a quite remarkable account and not fully explained in many English translations. This gem reveals that the tense in *moved upon the face of the deep* is inaccurate for the original reveals a descriptive continuance.

14

PILGRIM'S JOURNAL: Genesis 1:2

Our family farm was a pleasant place for residing and abiding. Among the many engaging interests of our happy "clan" were exploration of the island paradise to the south of the property, the towering pines drawing their nourishment from the adjacent, gently flowing stream to the east, the apple orchard and nearby cattle pastures to the north, and to the west, the home of our hens—our "chook yard".

Why introduce our "chook yard" to this expedition? We knew the way of hens and chickens, of crowing roosters and of gathered eggs. Come back to the point? But that's where we are. Precisely where we are!

Genesis 1:2, if reading from the original Hebrew, clearly states: …*the ruach*—**Spirit of God**—*was moving… hovering… over the surface of the mighty oceans.*

To begin the spade work, it must first be discerned that here is no flat, past tense *moved* or *hovered*. There is a clear note of continuance in the text which should be registered. And here is the gem: it will be discovered in the thoughts engendered by *hovering*. A precise translation of this word will provide an even more explicit narrative: *the Spirit of God was* **brooding** *over the surface of the sea.*

Any chicken-farm child can explain the habits of a broody hen! To paraphrase the text, we may affirm that *the Spirit of God was readying the waters for the coming of life: moving, hovering, brooding, ready to nurture elementary life!*

The Holy Spirit is here introduced as the Spirit of Life. Already, God was preparing for the coming of living creatures. The planet was soon to become a watery nursery.

What are we doing to assist in the continuance of life in this "chook yard" known as Earth? As we shall later observe: from its beginnings, humanity has been given a duty of care for all flora and fauna on the planet. Climate change—global warming—looms as one of the greatest challenges in history.

HIDDEN TREASURE: *LIGHT*

Sunrise will waken the dawn to overwhelm the night and grant light.

A WORD FROM THE WORD

aor – "light"

Oh, the brilliance of that first dawn! Darkness had dwelt upon the *face of the deep*. But light—*aor*—will always overcome darkness. The scene was possible because light had dawned upon the ocean. My camera has revealed the rolling back of the clouds of night across the sky. The light has come!

A VIEWPOINT TO PONDER
What is the difference between light and enlightenment?

What is light? Light is energy which is best described as electromagnetic radiation. It is not possible to obliterate light for where there is no matter, what can be destroyed? In view of this, how is it possible to explain–in a simple sentence–the nature of enlightenment? Here we are confronted with a comprehension of truth; it is understanding, it is **wisdom**.

PILGRIM'S JOURNAL: Genesis 1:3

In order to be "enlightened", it is necessary to allow the **light** of understanding and wisdom—wisdom being perhaps best interpreted as "the right application of knowledge"—to dawn!

It seems an appropriate time to take an initial foray into the reading of how the most ancient scribe would have set down the record in Hebrew. The descriptions provided beside the Hebrew alphabet on page 158 will allow the pictures to form. The language is read from right to left (incidentally, a dot is placed over the middle letter, *vav*, to provide the vowel *o*). To record *aor*, then, we find the OX, then the HOOK, then the HEAD. What may the "Picture Parables" reveal from the most ancient "script"? *The predominant One holds secure and leads.*

Light will always be predominant over darkness! Life would be possible now that the light would shine upon the Earth! Light will always reveal the pathway ahead!

So, back to the extant record before us now: Genesis 1:3

> *And God said, 'Let the light shine!' and there was light.*

Is the word *bara* to be detected here? No! The materials, the sun, moon and stars had already been created—*in the beginning…* What did happen? God said, *Let the light shine* and behold: the dawn! The most natural turn of events here was that the clouds had rolled back, allowing the sun to stream forth its light to strike the "face" of Earth for the very first time!

Marvel at the wisdom of the ancients. They got it right: first the materials for here is the universe. This enabled the light then to shine upon Earth's mighty oceans. Following on, in logical sequence, life was created and then enabled to emerge under the good hand of God! Light made it possible for life!

> *Light is shining, ever shining, on the sacred page;*
> *Bearing Truth's illumination, answers for our age.*

> *Light that shimmers on our sadness, turn our night to day;*
> *Light that glistens on our gladness, let us shine, we pray.* (LLT)

HIDDEN TREASURE: *DAY*

The sun's "clock" never needs re-winding.

A WORD FROM THE WORD

יוֹם
yom - "day"

By following on with a further translation of the most ancient, original Hebrew, some remarkable discoveries could be discerned. Always reading "backwards", from the right to left, we find the *yod*: *hand*—followed by the *vav* (transformed to the vowel *o* by a dot): the *hook*—then the final form of *mem*: the *ocean at rest*. Remarkable thinking! Here is the Hand of God who grants us security and peace! Is this what your day holds?

A VIEWPOINT TO PONDER
Why does day begin at a "breath" past 12 midnight?

It should be said, of course, that a decision regarding TIME would be fraught with far more complexities if settled on the moment when the sun first revealed its daily glow in the near environs of our own homes, but what of the inevitable seasonal changes? GMT: Greenwich's world clock becomes plausible!

PILGRIM'S JOURNAL: Genesis 1:3

How long is a *yom*? A *yom* is a **day** (commencing at evening). therefore "24 hours" is the set time zone. All things would be thrown out of kilter if one could modify in any way, the time of a day. Time is set by the unerring movement of the Earth's sphere as it progresses in its annual course through our particular portion of the universe, taking exactly 365¼ days each year.

24 hours has served Earth well since time immemorial. A day is a day: that is—inevitably—24 hours; unless, a "day" could mean something entirely different! Have I not been heard to say in unmistakable terms, when some silly new fad lands on the "horizon": 'this would not have happened in my day!' How long was that supposed "day"? Does this not mean that the term can be used metaphorically? Or, even to be set poetically?

Genesis 1 requires closer scrutiny. It requires some spadework. What is it saying and, how is its truth being expressed? How could the universe and all its glorious height and depth and length and breadth have been brought into existence in just six days? With God, all things are possible. However, 6 days is improbable, unprovable! Science—with irrefutable evidence it appears—will attest that it is impossible!!!

What is Genesis 1 claiming? In six days, God created the universe, including Earth. Yes! But in what form is the text being presented? Genesis 1 may be read as the Hebraic form of poetry! While Hebrew poetry fails in the basic forms of rhyme and rhythm, it abounds in the modes of antithesis, acrostics, paraphrase, question and answer, progression, and repetition!

Look again at Genesis 1: *the evening and the morning were the 1st, 2nd, 3rd, 4th, 5th, 6th, and 7th days.* And also: the repetition of *…it was good.* The scribe who set down the staggeringly accurate aspects of creation, did so in impeccable poetry! He could just as well have used the alternates *…the 1st, 2nd, 3rd … season, age* or *eon*! Oh yes, Genesis 1 allows for the scientific mind to agree with the poetic "turn of phrase" in this unique record! Scientific principles and data abound in this text!

DISCOVERED TREASURE: *DAYS*

And God said, 'Let there be Light!' And there was Light!

A WORD FROM THE WORD

יוֹמִים

yomim – "days"

One might say, "It was 'out-of-this-world!'" Yes, to be above the clouds in the glorious morning light. The experience was superb. Then, the clouds rolled back to reveal—coming out of the darkness of night—the beautiful Isle of Tasmania, the home of my birth. I came to think of that morning as akin to the first of mornings: it was when the clouds rolled back to display God's handiwork, that the calendar began. The distinguishing of day from night: *Let there be light!* allowed Earth's time to begin.

A VIEWPOINT TO PONDER
Is that all there was? Four words, and time begins?

Here was Eternity touching Time! Here was God giving the light something to shine upon. The clouds rolled back to display the beauty of each passing night and day. And behold, it was good!

PILGRIM'S JOURNAL: Genesis 1

It is high time we returned to the dawn of Earth where **Eternity touches Time**! Impossible! Of course. What I meant to say was, let us turn back the pages of the Bible's record of earliest history and observe, again, Genesis 1:2 where we have found the first tabulation of the word "DAY": the Hebrew, יוֹם or, if in the plural form: יוֹמִים. The reason for this checking out the original text in its most ancient form is to again invite a scanning of the Hebrew alphabet—in its most ancient form—on page 158, to discover that the word translated as **days** provides us with the hand, the hook, the raging ocean, then again, the hand. The day is complete with the ocean at peace. What a gem!

Wonderful, really. The LORD did not just speak the words: He had a Hand in all that was accomplished; He held all things together; He was aware of the raging ocean: there came His Hand once more. And then: the ocean became calm and all was peaceful, ready for the first evening that moved on into the first morning. Yes: the calendar had begun! The sense of continuance: night, then day… night… day…

How many nights, how many days, of incalculable time elapsed before the coming of "The Second Day" when the dry land appeared from the ocean depths? We may never know. God's "calendar" has ALL things in place, from before the beginning to after the end! He IS "The Aleph and the Tav" or more in keeping with our parlance: He IS "the Alpha and Omega"! In both the Hebrew and the Greek renditions, the words mean: He IS "The Beginning and the End."

The night, the day, are wonderful gems. They were given freely to each person who has ever populated Earth—some, on Easy Street, others in abject poverty. Perhaps the night and the day are the best of all gifts placed in our hands by the One who gave us LIFE to enjoy, and make good use of each, and every day!

How do you utilise these wonderful gifts, these gems stemming from the earth—the Earth—where we were given birth? How do you cherish these gems? Get in touch with God. Tell Him!

HIDDEN TREASURE: *HUMANITY*

The expression of Love… Joy… Peace… comes from the heart.

A WORD FROM THE WORD

אדם   חוה
adam "Adam"   *eve* - "Eva"

As we have observed on a previous occasion, names are chosen for a variety of reasons. Whatever the reasons for the naming of my dear friends, David and Grace, their parents could not have been more accurate: I introduce you to David—*beloved*—and Grace—*kind, thoughtful, pleasant, generous.*

A VIEWPOINT TO PONDER
What may a name reveal?

Adam was the first of humankind? In fact, he was among the first of humankind. He was one of the species named "**man**". It is most interesting to see, from Genesis 1:26, that, when God announced: *Let US make man in OUR own likeness,* the word employed is **adam**! The text continues: *and let THEM lead… God created man both male and female.* Both, known as MAN!

PILGRIM'S JOURNAL: Genesis 1:26

The spade has unearthed some intriguing data. Adam is not quite what a surface scan of Genesis may convey! It is also somewhat illuminating to discover that the Hebrew words for man and for woman are, essentially, the same: איש (man), contains the *aleph, yod,* and *shin.* Hmm: *predominant one, hand upon everything, with guardian responsibilities*!

Next, אשה, (woman), will set us back on our seats: It is the same—with a final *window* to *view* the feminine variety of man! That same *window* (observe the final letters of both "Eva" and "woman": the letter ה is used at the end of a word to denote the femininity of a person or object). A gem: "woman" is constructed with no inferior materials to those utilised in the creation of a man: we are all, precisely, created as integral representatives of the species known as **humanity**!

There is good reason for such a detailed analysis of this seemingly simple matter. Why must so many cultures hold to a patriarchal society that treats the female variety as no better than slaves, trampled under-foot? It is time that ALL woke up!

When next we meet Adam in the text, we will observe that the general term: *adam* has evolved into "Adam". Here then, is an actual man who has been named Adam. The meaning of his name, however, remains basically the same though, to be precise, the more descriptive term *red earth* may be attached. It is correct. After all, *we are dust, and to dust we shall return.*

With the introduction of the highest form of creation—humankind—Genesis 1 (that great Hebrew poem which encompasses theological and scientific data), draws to a close. It has failed to speak in the scientific terminology of ages, eras, and eons, it is true. Yet the selection of "day", faulty though it may seem to most, none-the-less allows the text to set out in precise order, this magnificent presentation of the creation of the **universe**, the gifting of **life**, and the endowment of a **spirituality** that enables humanity to live through our years in accord with the express plan and purpose of *Elohim*—God.

HIDDEN TREASURE: *SANCTIFIED*

Flocks abiding in green pastures are satisfied if beside still waters.

A WORD FROM THE WORD

קדש
qadesh - "sanctify"

There is something very special about a scene that exudes a sense of peacefulness. Not a ripple on the stream, the flock at rest, one bending to slake its thirst. It seemed to my camera, able to capture the scene, that there was a blessing to be received here. It was Sunday morning and, having just returned from Church, Psalm 23 came readily to my mind. Has it to you?

A VIEWPOINT TO PONDER
What makes a Sunday different from the other six days?

At first, it was not the first—day, that is! Genesis 2:2 announces that, by the seventh day, God had completed His project of creating the universe. He rested from His task. Not that He was drained of energy! God was marking the time: the Sabbath!

PILGRIM'S JOURNAL: Genesis 2:3

Genesis 2:1–3 marks a turning in the trail: *The creation of the heavens and the Earth were completed. It was now the seventh day and God rested from His labour!*

When did Creation (or, "The Big Bang"), take place? Scientists attest, from their "encyclopaedic" data-gathering techniques, that some billions of years have passed since this stupendous event brought something out of nothing! Their findings emerge from a multitude of facts which cannot be denied. We may never know the exact date of "Day 1". What can the Bible tell us, then, that we do not already surmise?

Genesis 1 makes us aware of the acknowledged sequencing: the provision of **materials**, to the gifting of **life**, then the creation of a **soul** capable of communing with the Creator! Though the later insertion of chapters breaks the flow of the Creation saga, the grandeur of the poetic *Master*-piece of Genesis 1 is given its grand finale in Genesis 2:1–3.

Far from going to sleep on His majestic achievement, God pronounces a special blessing at the ending of "the week": God *blesses* the 7th day. This question could well have been placed in "A Viewpoint to Ponder", though its entry in this pilgrim's journal provides an apt benediction: what is the true meaning of the word "blessing"? It is the bestowal of Divine favour and, to further assist our understanding, some synonyms: to anoint, dedicate, hallow, invoking joy and peace.

Then, to provide the ultimate gem, God **sanctified** the 7th Day! Yes, this question must also be asked: what does it mean to be "sanctified"? The key synonym here is to be holy. And, what does it really mean to be "holy"? It means to be pure, saintly, sacred, to be separated from anything that would spoil one's devotion. Saintly? While still alive on Earth? William Barclay, that great Scottish theologian, says it best: "To be holy is to be different and to make a difference." The pilgrim is one who can make discoveries hidden from the tourist trekking through the years, treading the superficial soils of circumstance.

THE REFLECTIVE GLANCE

A PILGRIM'S QUESTION: 'WHAT DOES
THE REALITY OF A TRINITY OF BEING TEACH ME ABOUT
MY TRUE IDENTITY', MAY BE ANSWERED HERE:

THE CRUCIAL ANALYSIS

Say, what am I? A cosmic accident?
Atomic particles, conveniently aligned,
And harmonised with earth?
A watery womb, by Intricate Design,
Took DNA via genes and chromosomes,
To helix frames: the key to life.
A game of chance? A Masterpiece
That birthed this child, uniquely me.

Say, who am I? Mere animated mud?
A body taking sustenance from sand,
Composed of dust made moist within
A pregnant womb? Intelligent Design
Has gifted wisdom to a matrixed form.
Does this analysis prove soil or soul?
I'm fathered by a Mastermind,
An Architect Supreme created me.

Say, why am I? A peerless plan?
What does it mean, to be connected to
All life, yet move a mind beyond
The womb of apes? Inspired Design
Has breathed discerning faculties
In me: I know, and know I know:
I've found the purpose schemed!
It lends Eternity to soil: to me!

Poems, p. 5, 26, first published by International Society of Poets. Copyright: author.

This pilgrim must acknowledge the wonder that arises in the soul at the greatness, the glory, and the grandeur of Creation by confirming that God's continuing love, nurture, guidance and grace have brought about the re-setting of life's purpose—goal.

THE FORWARD GLANCE

WHAT ARE LIFE'S POSSIBILITIES FOR "MAN"?
WE WERE CREATED FOR ETERNITY AND OUR WEARY
SOULS WILL FIND NO SERENITY UNTIL WE KNOW GOD'S
PEACE INVADING OUR CURRENT CIRCUMSTANCE.

* WONDERFUL!

From Psalm 103: Tune: *Calabar*

Wonderful, the LORD of Creation,
For His beauty outshines the stars;
Darkness is going, morning is glowing,
Night shall depart and morning arise.
Sun on the mountain, dew in the valleys,
Now I can see His glorious light
Wak'ning the Earth, and I will praise Him
For this miracle of sight.

Wonderful, the dawn of Creation,
When the world's first day was born;
Fountains are flowing, flowers are growing,
Splendid the sunrise in this new dawn.
Adam and His LORD communing,
Lions with lambs they won't annoy,
This was God's Eden and I will thank Him
For this miracle of joy!

Wonderful, God's new Creation,
Far beyond Earth's treasure trove;
Lofty the mountains, deep are the Earth's mines,
Higher yet, the scope of God's love,
Deeper still, the depth of His mercy!
Now I can see this with my own eyes,
Salvation's story and I adore Him
For this miracle of grace!

Mercy is mercy because we can expect God's "Helping Hand".
Grace is the greater for God desires to meet our need even
though we don't deserve it! Wonderful: *both* are available.

HIDDEN TREASURE: *HANDS*

The Peace of God surpasses human understanding.

A WORD FROM THE WORD

בְּיָדְךָ עִתֹּתַי

b'yardak atthi – "In Your Hand (are) my times"

The paucity of my ability to transcribe Hebrew words into English is seen here. As best I can, I have endeavoured to articulate the words of Psalm 31:15, *My times are in Your Hand.* There is good enough reason to make the effort. My depiction of "PEACE" painted on a satin drape may paint the world as it came to be when the land first rose pristine from the ocean bed.

A POINT TO PONDER
Does this mean the time was right for humankind?

The time is right when humankind reaches out for God's Peace. Our peace? Absence of strife; God's peace calms the strife!

PILGRIM'S JOURNAL: Genesis 2:1 – 7

The juxtaposition of Psalm 31:15 with the Gems to be found in Genesis is surely when humankind first walked among the splendours of Eden! The third and final creation—the human soul: humankind's capacity to communicate with God and our ability to discern right from wrong—Adam, met and shared his daily experiences of Eden with God. They walked hand in Hand!

The reading of the most ancient Hebrew script will allow a greater understanding of what our present focus presents. Turn with me to page 158 to behold, in relation to *our times are in God's Hand*—reading from right to left—the *house* (we are sheltered), the *hand* (we are held), the *door* (we are given freedom to choose), the *open hand*—final form, (God is ready to help us). Then, the *eyes* (His eyes are upon us), and the last letter in the alphabet: the sign—doubled for affirmation—the *cross*! The final letter affirms the truth of TAV: my days, my situation, my hopes, times: ALL in God's **Hand**! Here's the gem!

In my book, "*Apocalypse Dawn*" these two lists are to be found under the title "The Resolution of the Ages". We have been speaking of the "Alpha and Omega": this present study finds an appropriate time to share "The Beginning and The End"

The Beginning	The Ending:
Creation of the Universe	Re-creation of heavens and Earth
"Let there be Light!"	"God is Light"
Creation of life	Living existence transformed
Creation of humankind	Re-creation of humankind
Innocence in Eden	Purity in Paradise
Humankind living in Eden	Humankind living in Paradise
Fellowship with God	God dwells with humankind
Tree of Life. Trees: good/evil	Tree of Life freely accessible
Satan enters the garden	Satan is vanquished
Humankind succumbs to sin	Sin is eradicated
Exclusion from Eden	Humankind living in Paradise
Separation from God	Perfect harmony with God

What is the single, most important sign in history that, finally, rights the wrongs of human history? The tav: *THE CROSS!!!*

HIDDEN TREASURE: *YHVH*

Truth will not remain hidden. The Light draws out its validity.

A WORD FROM THE WORD

יהוה
yhvh - "*Jehovah*"

It was the journey to the Dead Sea that made it possible. To have stood on the brow of a nearby hill at Qumran gazing at those caves was quite awe-inspiring. Fleeing the marauding forces of Rome that were intent on obliterating Israel from the map of history, the *Essenes*—the guardians of their ancient scrolls of the Torah and related scriptures—placed them in the safety of the caves at Qumran. This priceless treasure was unearthed accidentally by a shepherd boy in 1947. The *Essene* scrolls had been lost for approximately 2,000 years.

A VIEWPOINT TO PONDER
What do the Dead Sea Scrolls tell the world today?

What do these ancient scrolls convey? The modern Bible is aligned with the ancient text. Well done, earliest scribes! Your copying skills affirm the validity of God's Word—the Bible—that modern printing presses reproduce so effectively today.

PILGRIM'S JOURNAL: Genesis 2:4

A strategic change has taken place in the narrative. Genesis 1 has described, via the specialised mode of poetry, a definitive—though generalised—record of the creation of the universe. Genesis 2 introduces us to the formation of the Hebrew people whom we know today as the Jews.

Having already transitioned from the tourist to the pilgrim—a traveller intent on pursuing a well-defined goal—I take my leave of Genesis 1–2:3 where precious gems have already been unearthed. An adjacent site beckons in the search for further Gems in Genesis.

Before taking up the spade, you may ask me to explain the nature of my personal goal. It is to finally meet face to Face in Eternity with the Person whose Identity has been disclosed. Genesis 2:4 will inform us of the One who dwells beyond time and space yet is readily accessible to all who call Him LORD (always capitalised to denote the unique nature of this Name).

The Guide Book takes on a new emphasis. We have already met with humankind—both varieties, male and female—and how a man is formed especially by *Elohim*: God. His name will be, unsurprisingly, Adam. And, be it noted, Adam as yet has no suitable companion! Amazing things are about to unfold!

God, now reveals Himself by the Name beyond all names! Here is *Jehovah*, or—nearer to the actual—*Yahweh*. We have approached the meeting place of the One who introduces Himself as *YHVH* or *YHWH*. Just four letters, known as "the Holy Tetragram" (4 letters, but they introduce *Yahweh* to our western mindset). Allow *Yahweh* to introduce Himself, explaining the actual tetragram. His declaration is: *I am "**I AM**".*

How, in all the realms of reality, can this Name tell us anything about the **LORD**? Actually, it is profoundly simple! *YHVH* (preferred), dwells in Eternity though nearer to all who call Him LORD than our breathing: "*I AM* in The Past, Present, Future!" *YHVH* **IS**!—there are no time or space limitations with YHVH!

HIDDEN TREASURE: *THE GARDEN OF EDEN*

A garden will bring pleasure to the eye and joy to the heart.

A WORD FROM THE WORD

גו   עדו

gan - "garden"   *eden* - "Eden"

A tourist may well include the great gardens of the world on the "bucket list" and many come to mind. The Botanical Gardens in Singapore, the Butchart Gardens in Canada, and Kew Gardens in London rank among the most superb. In the hills near my home is the Rhododendron Garden to the east of Melbourne. These magnificent blooms provide a "carpet" of colour

A VIEWPOINT TO PONDER
What, really, is a garden?

A garden is considered an enclosed space that is nurtured, bringing pleasure. The garden may include flowers, fruit, or vegetables. Whatever, that garden will require knowledge regarding climate factors, planning, planting, and hard labour!

PILGRIM'S JOURNAL: Genesis 2:8

How very interesting! The Hebrew word *gan* is basically comprised of the first and last letters of the English translation: *garden.* Also, *Eden*—give or take the problem of vowels in the Hebrew—requires absolutely no translation for it is cognate.

Where was **Eden**? The Guide Book must be consulted here. Is there a map? The location is difficult to determine but the emphasis on the river could refer us to the Euphrates, flowing supremely through that eastern region now known as Mesopotamia. The associated river known as the Tigris would make the land between the two rivers wonderfully conducive to the planting of a bordered garden! The map also makes clear the fact that the two rivers commence as four streams which, in flowing south to the Persian Gulf, finally become the one river!

There has been some conjecture that the Nile River may be the focal point of Eden, in light of the fact that Cush is mentioned in the ancient text. The region of Cush is now widely regarded as Ethiopia, introducing Africa to the discussion. To this pilgrim's mind, however, the great expanse of territory thus involved tends to negate the theory. However, one should not easily displace the Nile's association with Egypt, still regarded as one of the most ancient countries of the world. And, there are thoughts of humanity first coming out of Africa.

A precious gem will arise as we continue to retrace our steps to the beginning of the human story. A later "dig" will help our deliberations. It involves the story of a man who lived in Ur of the Chaldees, which is reputed to have been a settlement near the Tigris and Euphrates Rivers that finally meet before flowing into the Persian Gulf. This man carried the genes of the Hebrew people, the progenitors of whom are Adam and Eve.

Yes! The borders of these two great rivers would have made the ideal place in which to plant a garden where the man— Adam (*of the red earth*)—could begin his appointment by *YHVH* to become a gardener! But there was a vital ingredient missing in Eden! What was it? A Gem?

HIDDEN TREASURE: *EARTH*

As the sun breaks through, the mountain will be seen in all its glory.

A WORD FROM THE WORD

אדמה
adamah – "Earth"

My paintbrush has managed to convey something of the beauty of my childhood home. This was a valley dominated by the towering peak of "Sleeping Beauty". Though "she" was asleep quite perennially, our mountain was the predominant feature of the valley. If you wish to see how "Beauty" lay, turn the painting to the vertical and you will see "her" there. There were many gems to be found in this valley: the river coursing down to meet the Southern Ocean, the apple orchards, vegetable patches, and the gardens, lovely gardens. Yes, there was beauty here, made so—basically—by the soil which supported life: all life!

A POINT TO PONDER
Why is the unseen soil so vital to the life of the earth?"

We must take stock of the unseen so we may value what is seen. Allow your "spade" to dig below the superficialities of life!

Have you noticed that the Hebrew language names **earth** as "adamah", *adam*, in the feminine mode? What of the English? We may sing of a tree: '… that lifts *her* leafy arms to pray… '

In these latter days of the creative process, that which is seen can appear so mundane. We've seen the scene so many times it fails to find a WOW, let alone a thoughtfulness to breathe 'thank You, LORD!' Take the soil—the earth of Earth. In searching for the gems to be unearthed in Genesis, I am prone to say, 'take your spade, dig below the superficialities of life for it is below the surface dirt that we will find life's true values.'

It is time to unearth the Earth! Observe the constituents of the soil we tend to trample on each day. Most will be more than surprised to know that about 25% of all that comprises earth is of the water component, give or take a shower or two. Another 25%, or there abouts? Wait for it… it is the air (not breathable, it is true), but the gases of the air are there, within the soil. What of the remaining 50%? All of 45% is composed of the minerals—there are 3 main commodities: sand, silt, and clay. This allows just 5%, give or take. The soil also accommodates the mouldering leaves, the worms and such like, for here we have the necessary organic matter.

No hard and fast rules can be applied, of course, for there are floods, and fires, and famine to consider in the mix. Also, some soils will receive the cactus and look after it, while other soils are more at home with ferns and forest giants. Most times, a seed will know just where to plant itself—it falls from its parent's pod!

Humanity depends upon this "mundane" conglomerate for the sustenance of life will depend on it. We tend to devalue this gem though its worth is beyond rubies, so to speak! How do we care for this, one of the earliest of God's gifts when forming the earth of Earth? We have not cared as we ought for the land which gave us birth. The deforestation of forests leaves us devoid of the roots that hold the soil together. Chemical fertilisers denude the landscape. And, we must retain a balance of soil and water!

A Gem – Adam

THE GARDENER

How beautiful, this Eden land!
Here is a garden where I walk
in step with Him, the LORD
who granted me this wonderful,
this perfect—Eden—home.

He comes to me, He talks with me,
He shares with me the wonders of
this precious place. He speaks
to me of all the mighty mysteries
the glorious universe displays;
a grandeur wrought each day
by His unique, creative power.
The LORD has taught me, Adam,
many things, He's near each day.
I hear His voice: He calls to me,
He whispers too. I hear
Him audibly and, in my heart.

This is my home! And yet I know
it is God's land. He's gifted me
with ground to till, to nurture, and
to coax the tender plants to bear
with seasons as the sun ascends.
It warms the soil, gives colour to
the blossom, bud on bough,
and every fruit that's grown.

I am the gardener, I tend this land,
this pristine land. I also guide
the animals to placid streams.
I have responsibilities: there is
a purpose in my life. I know it to be so!
As evening nears, I rest from tasks
set out for me to tend each day.

THE GARDENER

I wait to hear the footfall of
His tread within this vale
where every tree and flower
lend perfume to the wafted air.
The LORD will tarry with me here
to teach life values—what it means
to love, to trust, to walk in grace.
I'm learning what faith means.
I see Him not as we converse
but know His smiling Face!
Yes, there is much to learn—
I am so innocent. And here,
He speaks His will to me:

And now, the YHVH–LORD
is near: He brings to me a bride!
What greater gift than this
could He bestow? My Eve!
Here is the other half of me!
I am complete for now my Eve
is bone of bone and flesh of flesh
of me. And, we will love always
as "one" in every way. I'll live
to please my Eve and care for her
as God requires. I hear Him now.

... you are a triune being and
so like the Triune Elohim.
Discern the consequence of choice,
ensure your body, mind, and soul
are whole. There is a given way
for humankind to rise to the
Eternal Home of God.

I'll need to keep in mind,
remember, all the truths
that YHVH–LORD has taught!

HIDDEN TREASURE: *KNOWLEDGE*

A garden becomes a garden by tender, loving care

A WORD FROM THE WORD

דַּאַת

daath - "knowledge"

To relax in a garden can be what may be termed soul renewing. It is the absorption of beauty, the investigation of a leaf—its shape and dimension, one in a multitude of varieties to ponder: a frond; a branch; a tree. It is the joy of seeing a rose come into bloom, to catch its scent, to observe the busy bees about their particular responsibilities, to acknowledge the endeavours of the gardener, and find an arbour in which to abide in peace.

A VIEWPOINT TO PONDER
What is the difference between a wilderness and garden?

Look over the fence. Observe the wayside weeds, the tight tangle of the rushes and vines, untrained growth, shrubs struggling for water, fertilisation, and space to live without want. The wilderness holds possibilities but it needs a gardener.

PILGRIM'S JOURNAL: Genesis 2:8–9

Having reached Gen. 2:8–9, what a shock! A scan of the Hebrew word for "**knowledge**" hears the "sound" of death: *daath* cannot mean what its Hebrew letters seem to convey. It will be noted that the letter *tav* appears at the end of the word though, when placed anywhere but the initial letter, which is aided by a central dot, *"t"* is pronounced *"th"* so, the sound is right! To be precise, the two words are but an unfortunate juxtaposition. A later survey will give another "take" on the term, but the words do not mean the same. Yet the matter cannot be dropped.

"*The Crucial Analysis*" poem, page 26, has emphasised a key aspect of knowledge that must not pass us by. The truth of the relevant line is drawn from the nature of the 3rd creation—that where **meaning** is added to the earlier miracles of the creation of **matter**, then of **motion**: life! Humankind was blessed with the capacity to "know, and know that we know". We are not walking encyclopaedias, knowing everything there is to know. But we are gifted with a discernment between right and wrong.

Via another language—Latin—a most descriptive word expresses the truth of what my poem seeks to convey. The word is "conscience". To unravel the mystery, the prefix *con* is used to convey the idea of togetherness: to be with, to be side by side; and the all-too familiar 2nd portion of the word—*science*—actually means "knowledge". Con-science? This is a knowledge BESIDE knowledge! It is a capacity born in the spirituality of humankind that enables us to determine the value of accepting or declining an idea or a deed! It is possible for us to hear a *related* knowledge within giving counsel to knowledge in deciding the right or wrongness of a thought or action.

In light of the gifting of conscience to humankind as the culmination of the creative programme of *Elohim* to crown creation with a spirituality, it most definitely is not "conscience" that was the "missing ingredient" in Eden! Adam was blessed with the ability to determine the rightness or wrongness of any and all of his thoughts and his actions in Eden! This is a Gem!

HIDDEN TREASURE: *TREES*

Some trees may not provide the nurture promised

A WORD FROM THE WORD

עֵץ
aits – "tree"

Two trees growing side by side from the moment of "birth" yet these trees give vastly different accounts of what lies under the bark. A tree is always true to itself. To the left, a fine sapling with bark almost shed to show the inner quality of pure white wood! Adjacent is a most "welcoming" tree with a branch made ready for the weary traveller to sit awhile. The traveller "hears" its invitation but a pilgrim will test the veracity of the "seat" first!

A VIEWPOINT TO PONDER
When could a tree be a negative influence on a life?

Trees may be taken as an illustration to prove a point. This pilgrim tends to speak of such as a "Picture Parable". It has been wisely said that a picture is worth a thousand words. Just so, if the "visual aid" of a tree reminds anyone of a quality of life. Let it represent the truth to be observed and absorbed.

PILGRIM'S JOURNAL: Genesis 2:9

A superficial scan of the Genesis account of *In The Beginning…* appears quite banal to modern eyes and ears. There is most certainly good enough reason to make such an assessment. Think of the "days" (!), the years, the ages, which have intervened through which humanity has amassed such a development in intellect, understanding, and the expanding memory bank. This serves us well when detecting the naivety of the data confronting the would-be Genesis pilgrim.

It is appropriate to interrogate the records! The realities of right and wrong are far more serious than to attribute, to a couple of "**trees**", the best and the worst news to be found recorded in today's daily newspapers, or presented on the hourly newscast! Surely there is a better rendition of the nature of right and wrong than those two trees presenting themselves as the reason for all the miracles and maladies that have beset humankind throughout the on-going centuries without relent!

What, actually, has been revealed by pointing out the stark contrast in the veracity, the virtue, the value, the valour, the validity, of a good decision? When set against the vice, the vanity the villainy, the vehemence, the venal, the vexed, the vicious, the vile, the violent and the vulgar that wrongful attitudes and actions introduce, goodness is plain to see.

Adam was in "kindergarten", He was preparing for his "school-days". The teacher of an early learning class will employ examples of the subject to be taught by utilising visual aids— from simple sketches to elaborate structures—the tools by which the truth is taught, the answers found. The effectiveness of what is taught is discovered in what is learned and is seen in the accumulation of knowledge and how it is applied to the life.

The "Picture Parables" of Genesis are quite remarkable, having stood the test of time by the realisation that the pictures portrayed are a visualised example of right and wrong. But there was still something missing—a vital ingredient—in Eden! Whatever could be missing in God's perfect garden?

HIDDEN TREASURE: *SOLITUDE*

It is possible to be lonely in a crowd and colour highlights the scene.

A WORD FROM THE WORD

לבד

lavad – "alone"

There is a massive difference between the state of being alone and the despair of loneliness. A person can feel most lonely when surrounded by a separate community of like-minded people. Any difference in outlook tends to raise unseen but recognised barriers denying hope of an affinity of friendship. It is perhaps pertinent to point out that the lonely swans at the front and the back of this bevy are garbed in a contrasting suit of feathers: both are black swans—the cause for separation?

A VIEWPOINT TO PONDER
How may colour and racial barriers be broken?

Change the view-finder, the spectacles of discrimination, and conquer fear of the unknown, incapacity to open dialogue! Many fail to realise that those feared also fear, so fail to communicate. A smile, a kindness, can break down barriers!

PILGRIM'S JOURNAL: Genesis 2:18–26

Here was Adam, working from dawn to dark... Well not quite, for there was another, special activity on his daily "to do" list. Adam took time out to discuss the daily happenings in Eden. With whom could Adam converse if living in **solitude** in Eden? Adam had unfettered access to *YHVH*. It is rather poignant to find that *YHVH* had asked Adam to name the creatures he came across in his daily toing and froing. Whatever the name suggested, that was the name applied.

While there is need to translate the names, for obvious reasons, it is possible to ascertain the nature of the beasts roaming through the environs of Eden. There would be the ox, (the supreme beast), and the sheep with its lambs, no doubt a camel or two and many others. Adam saw the various creatures finding their mate, saw the lambs emerging from the ewe, saw the joy that was expressed as mother fed her lamb and father shielded them from any looming danger in their grassy home. Oh yes, it was not good that Adam should be alone!

The most awesome and mysterious of all the "Picture Parables" found in Genesis is, most surely, the account of Adam falling into a deep sleep and, while "under that anaesthetic", a rib was extracted by the "Surgeon", *YHVH*, from his side! Now, a parable gains its title from the *para* portion of the word, granting a visualisation, a picture, of a truth that stands beside truth!

What, then, can the spade unearth from the text? What can be really happening here? The "Surgeon" is precise. He utilises his "knife" to extract a rib from Adam's side! Here is an obvious clue for deciphering the scene: Adam's bride would be at his side: bone not from the skull (to be the controller in the union, determining each course of action), nor from the feet (in order to be trampled under-foot)!

The truths discovered in Genesis 1 hold firm: humankind was created equal. The man and the woman are meant to stand side by side as ONE! It appears, to this pilgrim, that the ancient account is best read, and understood as a "Picture Parable" where lessons to be learned are recognised more easily.

HIDDEN TREASURE: *PRAYER*

A path will always be found where there is light ahead.

A WORD FROM THE WORD

אמר
amar – "speak"

Life can find one emersed in a forest, a jungle, when the problems confronting the traveller can become insurmountable. At times, an axe rather than a spade would appear to be the more appropriate tool or, dare I say weapon, when determining the way ahead. We need light! More profoundly, we need enlightenment. This path on Kangaroo Island leads to light.

A VIEWPOINT TO PONDER
How is it possible to hear an inner voice?

What does it mean to "hear"? In contemplating the question to hand, we can safely set the ears aside. One could not wisely consider the heart—the blood pump—to listen in. The word *heart* that we so blithely banter about can take on multiple meanings. Take for example, nature, feeling, love, affection, compassion. *Heart* has much to teach us! We need to listen in.

PILGRIM'S JOURNAL: Genesis 2:18

Genesis 2:18 has introduced the pilgrim to a new dimension in the qualities granted to this created being: the account of the formation of a man capable of communing with his Creator!

It is recorded here that *YHVH* spoke to Adam and Adam heard what was said! In fact, it was not an unusual occurrence. Adam was forming the habit of making this meeting with *YHVH* a daily imperative. **Prayer**: a gem? This is, truly, a diamond!

The pilgrim is not informed as to whether these conversations were verbal for, when it comes to prayer, it has been said that prayer is a simple exercise. It has been described as being akin to opening a door and entering this special space to commune with God—perhaps to place our petitions, our cares, before Him, or only to listen to the One who dwells in Eternity. It doesn't really matter which: just to acknowledge the Presence is prayer.

This most profoundly vital aspect of a person's experience of prayer has not changed. Those intent on prayer will be given access: the door will open, the *heart* finding a meeting place for speaking, and listening, to the One who still makes Himself available to the earnest seeker.

Most often it is the person seeking "audience" that does most, or all, of the speaking—the petitions, the intercessions, even before the thanksgiving for prayer answered, blessing granted, guidance given. But it is good to listen in to God!

We learn to wait awhile, in His Presence, finding comfort, encouragement, direction. The LORD is prone, even, to ask for our help!!! Someone comes to mind, an obvious need is recalled, a realisation is pressed in upon us that we can assist that struggling soul! What we need to do then is to ask for specific guidance, a pointing of the way and an acceptance of the means, of helping to fulfil the needs of another.

So, here we come upon Adam, communing with His Creator, his Counsellor, his Challenger. Adam is learning that he is not alone. But there is that vital ingredient still missing!

THE REFLECTIVE GLANCE

A PAUSE IN THE PROCEEDINGS OF
OUR DAILY LIVES ALLOWS FOR A GREATER
UNDERSTANDING OF GOD'S HANDIWORK.

* CREATOR GOD

Tune: *Come. ye thankful people* 7.7.7.7. D.

Glorious, the universe,
Stretching to the bounds of space:
Sun and moon each share their light,
Planets trek their ordered course.
Nebular and stellar flight
Heeds the power of God's commands,
For creation works as planned;
In each sphere we see God's Hand.

Beautiful, the scenes of Earth:
Snow-clad mountains, azure skies,
Landscapes sloping to the seas,
Valleys sing as rivers rise.
In the clouds, refreshing rain
For the harvest fruits' demands;
Flora, fauna, forest homes,
In each clime we view God's land.

Wonderful, creation's art,
Every pattern pertinent;
Each unique in its own right,
Its design most eloquent.
Genes and chromosomes grant style,
Helix frames hold every strand;
Set, the DNA is sealed:
In each form we find God's brand.

Marvellous! All life displays
Gifts of God through grace always;
All the Earth will hear our voice,
Day and night we speak our praise.
Now in hope our hearts rejoice,
Knowing truth will show its hand.
We will sing creation's song:
In the end, God's word will stand!

THE FORWARD GLANCE

IN CONSIDERING THE FIRST AGE OF EARTH,
THE PRISTINE NATURE OF THE UNIVERSE:
THE PURPOSE OF PRAYER IS ALREADY EVIDENT,
ITS POWER IS PROFOUND, AND ITS PROVISION
IS LIMITLESS. GOD'S GIFTING IS ABUNDANT
AND OFFERED FREELY TO ALL.

* SHINE, LIGHT OF GOD

Shine, Light of God, in the depths of the soul,
Come LORD, and make me whole;
Shine, Light of God, and illumine the mind,
Help me Your will to find.
Shine in my life today,
Shine in my heart, I pray,
For always I'll walk in the light of Your word,
That I may live for God.

Shine in this world, LORD, dispelling the night,
Shine in Your glorious might;
I look to You as the Light of the world:
Turn all my gloom to gold.
You are life's shining ray,
I would Your word obey;
O LORD, for my gladness draw near as I pray,
Turn all my night to day.

Now may I be, through Your own precious word,
Known as a child of God;
All who believe in Your own holy Name,
Now may affirm this claim:
You are the LORD of Light,
YHVH, You gave the right
For all to be known as God's children, it's plain,
When we are born again.

The miracle of creation, and re-creation, is not complete until the discovery is made that humankind is still granted access to The LORD—*YHVH*—today. Creation's date is impossible to determine but today's date is known and prayer is still actioned.

HIDDEN TREASURE: *LISTEN*

A tree that knows not its season provides no reason for its display.

A WORD FROM THE WORD

שׁמע
shamea – "Listen"

There was something wrong with that tree! I knew the season: it was spring! Why were there autumn leaves among the blossom? The tree had forgotten to release itself from autumn and, it had missed a whole season when its boughs should have been bare. This tree had failed to listen to the seasons. It had failed to listen to the source of its life—the sun, the shadows and, its roots. All too often, the human "tree" fails to listen to the Voice of Wisdom, of God, and know the good and the ill of life.

A POINT TO PONDER
Why should humankind always depend on its "roots"?

The alternative is isolation. From whence comes the soul's sustenance without the voice of reason, of guidance, of God? Oh yes, it is vital that we learn to listen. What do we hear?

PILGRIM'S JOURNAL: Genesis 3

How do we hear? A good question. And, more to the point, with what do we hear? With the ears, of course! But that is not all. We may dull, with hand over ears or by loud blaring music, the sound of a voice we do not wish to hear. However, there is another voice—that not carried by ordinary means and caught by the ears. It is the voice of conscience. Our prior reading of Genesis 2:8-9 will have introduced us to the word and its etymology: *con*: with, *science*: knowledge = knowledge beside knowledge. Or, to be more precise: a knowing beside knowledge. It requires the "ears" of the soul to hear that "voice"!

It is one thing to **listen**; it is quite another to HEAR! What does this require? Perhaps the ancient Hebrew can give us aid yet once again. What do we find from the list provided on page 158? The *guard*—discern what is heard and act accordingly. The raging *ocean*—does one face or flee from danger? Then, the *eyes*—what do we see? We are now well informed by our inner voice as to how we decide: choose the right or, the wrong!

There has been a question lurking in the background, and it is time to solve the issue. What was missing in the lives of our first parents? Surely, in His formation of the human being, God had not forgotten a vital ingredient? On the contrary, creation was now complete. And, humankind had been given the capacity to listen, both with ears and with soul! What could be missing? Eden provided the arena. What was yet lacking?

The tree would provide the answer! There was, in Eden, "the tree of good and evil". The tree in the picture provided held no fruit. It is enough to observe both autumn and spring on the bough. Yes, there was something wrong with that tree.

Whatever the "Picture Parable" represented in Eden's "tree", it provided a way for a choice to be made. Would Eve or Adam yield to the temptation offered by that so-called "tree" or, would they choose to turn from the evil offered? By their decision, they would gain the missing ingredient: EXPERIENCE. Would their decision strengthen, or weaken, them? We know the answer!

HIDDEN TREASURE: *TESTING*

A serpent, though clad with such magnificence, is deadly.

A WORD FROM THE WORD

נחש
nachash – "serpent"

Having been accosted by a snake impeding my preferred path, this pilgrim is aware of the dangers associated by "entertaining a serpent". However, when I speak of a "snake-in-the-grass", I do not refer to a slithering serpent. My adversary is otherwise, he or she may even be of the human variety, with satanic intent!

A PERTINENT POINT TO PONDER
How does one recognise a "snake-in-the-grass"?

The obvious answer is to recognise the guise! However, while it is easy to recognise a snake, there are insidious influences which look nothing like a serpent, sliding across the path to entrap unwary travellers—particularly those in search of a thrill.

PILGRIM'S JOURNAL: Genesis 3

We have arrived at a dramatic turn of events occasioned by the entrance of a serpent. A snake? The 2nd chapter of Genesis has been closed. Chapter 3 opens on an entirely new scene. Oh, Adam and his Eve were still residing in Eden but the text reveals what it is that has been missing, the vital ingredient that must be encountered, not only by Adam and his Eve, but by all who walk the trails and the trials, presented by life!

There will be the mountain-peaks of success, of achievement; the valleys of grief; the vast plains of disappointment; the desert lands of an arid existence that offers sparce refreshment for body, mind and soul. But there will also be the vistas of beauty where peace settles on the heart. This is what renews our will to continue the journey.

The missing vital ingredient that had intrigued the traveller thus far, as we have discovered, is the dire necessity of experience. There is only one way to gain experience. It will not be found in the tales told by others or in any text-books offering guidance. Experience must be experienced! *YHVH* was not going to hand it all to Adam and his Eve on a plate, so to speak. Adam and Eve needed to be confronted with situations that encouraged strengthening moral fibre, character, by exercising the innate gift within them to discern what was right and what was wrong.

Temptation is not evil! Temptation, however, must be mastered—it is the "**testing** tool"! The only means of controlling a circumstance is to allow the conscience—that knowledge beside knowledge—to give the guidance necessary to find the strength to say "no" to invitations that have unfortunate consequences. Under the outer cladding that fascinates, is the urge to participate in an ill-considered plan that leads to failure.

What is the truth to be unearthed in this narrative? It is the revelation of the *modus operandi* of the tempter:
1st: The doubt offered   – *Did God really say… ?*
2nd: The denial of retribution   – *No, you will not die… !!*
3rd: The lure–an alternative gift – *You will be like God… !!!*

HIDDEN TREASURE: *THE FRUIT*

The apple, by any other name, would taste as sweet.

A WORD FROM THE WORD

טֹוב
tob – "Good"

רַע
rai – "Evil"

I knew this apple orchard, I plucked its fruit. The fruit was ripe, ready for harvest. These apples own a delightful name: they are known as the Delicious. The intriguing aspect of the apple tree is that it cannot, by its own nature, spawn another tree of the same ilk. The required fruit to be grown on a given tree is grafted in. It is the work of the winter to be ready for the spring.

A VIEWPOINT TO PONDER
Could the "tree" in Eden have been an apple tree?

From whence came the tree that granted the Delicious—or any other variety—the cultured cuttings to be grafted into the selected tree? The apple tree appears to fit the purpose, particularly if "delicious". But Eden's "tree" has another name!

What is good? To be good is to be in possession of virtuous qualities, to be devoid of negative attributes or actions, to be honest, pure, with no stain upon the character. The etymology of "good" proves that it is not the same word as "God" as each have differing sources. None-the-less, it can be said that God is good! All goodness is, indeed, derived from God!

What is evil? To be evil is to be wicked, immoral, corrupt, depraved, iniquitous, guilty. It is said that there are three aspects of evil in humanity: moral, physical, and metaphysical—the philosophy of being and knowing. It appears to this pilgrim that the three aspects which make us human are involved in this "trinity" of components: by becoming involved in wrongdoing, we have allowed the grime of it to taint our soul, our body, and our mind. Where is the gem? It is the realisation:

How did sin enter Eden? Certainly, it was not by the ungainly growth of an apple tree! The eating of any **fruit** was not what spoiled the Edenic existence. It was a suggestion! How, in the realms of reality, could a subtle suggestion cause such irretrievable havoc? One must go beyond the suggestion to the tempter. Who is it that is euphemised as a serpent, a "snake-in-the-grass"? We have come to know him—yes, him—as Satan: the "adversary". He has also accrued more appendages, e.g., Lucifer (once "the angel of "light"), the devil!

One of Satan's pet perks is to allow himself to be portrayed with the horns, fork, and scarlet suit! Satan has become a laughable creature. If seen in that suit in Eden, Satan could not possibly have attracted Eve, and later, Adam, to stop by the "tree of the knowledge of good and evil"—knowledge that has evolved from the theoretical to experiential. The right application of the theoretical would have consolidated purity.

Eve, however, was attracted. It seemed good—looked virtuous. The doubt was entertained, the denial was heard, the disaster was actioned. The "tree" is a "Picture Parable", the "visitor", a reality, the "fall", a catastrophe!

HIDDEN TREASURE: *OPPORTUNITY*

When one gate closes, another can open for the brave.

A WORD FROM THE WORD

פקח

paqa<u>ch</u> – "to open"

What opens up to opportunities beyond the gate? All certainly looks promising. However, if one is thrust suddenly from an ideal existence into the terrors of the unknown, the portent is fraught with fear of what might be, could be. But could it possibly be that a new garden can be carved out of the wilderness?

A VIEWPOINT TO PONDER
Why can the closing of a door be so daunting?

The closing of a door signifies, predominantly, two things. Unless one leaves in anger and is glad of escape, a closed-door spells regret, grief, isolation from the past, and loss. Then, when the face is turned towards the future, fear of the unknown, inadequacy, and dread can absorb the mind, the soul.

PILGRIM'S JOURNAL: Genesis 3:17–24

Where was the gem of **opportunity**? Look at the loss! What were the opportunities? What was the loss? Significant questions, each of which should be addressed. In search of the opportunities: what did Adam and Eve retain? The most important of these was the matter of communication with *YHVH*. While the tone of the conversations had altered, Adam was still able to pray! He responded to the Voice of *YHVH*.

Adam's prayer stemmed from the necessity of explaining his failure to abide by the parameters of purity. He had fallen into the trap set so insidiously by Satan. He had his excuse, of course: 'Eve made me do it!' But it was still possible for Adam to walk with God in a garden. It was a garden, however, that would be tended by the sweat of his brow! Life would be hard work and there was much to learn beyond Eden. There was a new form of prayer, a new garden in which to live. And, there was the opportunity to find answers for his new needs.

Why did Adam, and Eve, require clothes? There was no need to be clad in Eden. What made the difference? We are here presented with a new set of "Picture Parables".

It appears very likely that the nature of the wrongful act perpetrated in Eden was linked to an unnatural sexual act. The clearly expressed consequence of what so intrigued Eve, then Adam, in Eden was that Adam and his Eve woke up to the fact that they were naked! This was a new development, they now felt ashamed and this related to their bodies—obviously linked to the deed. Another factor was to be that childbirth would be fraught with pain. The consequence of wrong is related to a wanton disregard for the good, the benefit of self and of others.

So! What was lost? What was the factor—told as we are becoming more aware—in "Picture Parables"? Why was that "gate" closed, then guarded by Heaven? No one would ever enter Eden again. What was the facility granted to humanity in creation that could never be retrieved? It is profoundly simple: Humankind had lost the gift of innocence! Chapter 3 now ends.

HIDDEN TREASURE: *MOTHER*

From birth the branch is dependent on its mother.

A WORD FROM THE WORD

חוה   אם

chevah – "life"   *em* – "mother"

To hear Paul Robeson's recording, this morning, of Kilmer's classic song/poem reminded me of the beauty of trees in the most picturesque of terms. Alfred Joyce Kilmer died early in the 20th century but his words still find a resonance in my soul: There is no "*poem*" as lovely as a tree… with nests of robins at home in **her** hair… whose branches have been weighed down with snow… with the rain sustaining life… lifting arms to pray… What appeals to this writer as I set myself to sharing something of the depth of meaning in "Picture Parables" is the word "HER"!

A VIEWPOINT TO PONDER
What are the basic aspects of Motherhood?

It's quite like standing on both legs gifted to humans. No one can stand on the one for long. What, you ask, do the two represent? Mother will stand erect upon Privilege and Responsibility. Both are gifts, though one—responsibility—may cause an early limp!

What could be the colour of the gem that gleams before us today? The opal comes to mind: the red of blood granted to the infant; orange: the warmth of **mother's** care; yellow: the richness of the love spread so lavishly upon the babe; green: the gift of life; blue: the purity of the highest principles of life displayed; and purple: the "Royal" bond that none can break!

The Hebrew language lifts out many hidden treasures— particularly in its most ancient form, yet, never-the-less extant until about the 7th century BC. A glance at the alphabet's "pictures" translates so well the living image of motherhood!

In observing, first, *Eve,* in its first format: ח represents a fence: two posts becoming "one" by the railing! The central letter is ו: the hook; the child is held, connected to its mother. The ה is the "window" through which the mother will open to the child the joys, and also the challenges of life!

Em can also allow its worthy gem to come to the surface via means of its Hebrew origin. Already, the א has made its impact on our deliberations: the predominant one. Surely, Adam? The textual material expresses it differently. From the day of THEIR creation, man was formed in both the male and female varieties. Therefore, Eve—the mother—can rightly take the א (carrying the "e") and stand equal with her husband. Therefore, *mother* can rightly claim that equal, rather than a subservient, place with the father! The 2nd letter: מ is beautiful indeed as it grants the picture of a sea at peace: mother, at her best, brings peace to the babe, settling it comfortingly in her arms!

Eve, the mother, now must exercise both her privilege and her responsibility to nurture two boys. What joys, and sorrows, Eve and Adam took on as—together—they faced up to the responsibilities of raising their two children. So disparate were those boys! It lifts the question, from the earliest of times, as to why those boys turned out so differently. Many, many, are the times when parents—who have done their best, given their best—encounter grief in the face of recalcitrance and defiance.

HIDDEN TREASURE: *FAMILY*

Proximity does not equate with communication.

A WORD FROM THE WORD

הבל   קין

hebel – "breath"   *cain* – "acquire"

How strange, that siblings should go through life as strangers though living in the same home! Nature has it that kinship would relate to kindred-ship. There are, however, intrusions into the mindset that negate any desire to communicate with those who sit at table to partake of the family repast, or lounge around to discuss the happenings of the day and the aspirations desired.

A VIEWPOINT TO PONDER
How may two turn face-to-face for the benefit of both?

What is the purpose of a face-to-face encounter? Is it amicability, problem-solving, for example? Or, is it to demand one's rights? Allow a little consideration for the others' circumstance, recognise a selfishness, a jealousy, and solve it. How may a shepherd and a farmer live in harmony? Be kind!

PILGRIM'S JOURNAL: Genesis 4:8–14

What was Cain's problem? Cain was jealous, vindictive. Things had been much to his liking as a child, before the intrusion of that blubbing babe on his happy homelife. Cain observed that he was no longer the centre of attention. The baby demanded that Mother turn from him to feed the baby brat!

Matters did not improve as Cain and Abel grew up, always with diverse interests and responsibilities. Father and Mother had "schooled" both boys to attend to their duties and to live in accord with the requirements of **family** life. Of paramount importance was the acceptance of the place that *YHVH* held in every aspect of life and living. That is, Cain and Abel were disciplined in the ways in which a sense of worship and its ramifications guided the family's intent to retain an innate goodness in thought, word, and deed: this is the gem!

Cain was a farmer; Abel cared for the family's flock. The parents had impressed upon the boys the need to return a portion of their earnings to *YHVH* as an act of worshipful gratitude for every way He had cared for them, led them, nurtured them, blessed them. The gift of a lamb was surely a precious gift that *YHVH* would appreciate. What could Cain lift from the earth to serve as sacrifice?

Cain was perturbed. He liked it not! Abel's lamb was far more valuable than his sheaf of wheat! 'I've many more in the barn—enough and to spare—but why should I deny myself by gifting excessive sacrifice when I have worked my fingers to the bone to make the best of it all? And, now, I must deprive myself of enough to balance out the worth of the lamb?' Cain would not be the last to query the need for expressing thankfulness!

When what appears to be a logical and well devised scheme is not found to be suitable is entertained to feed the grievance, jealousy can fester, mount in intensity, and lead to an inevitable conclusion. Cain rids himself of the problem: Abel! Where is Abel? His blood will cry out from the ground. Adam and Eve are bereft! How can Cain find, live with, a regret?

HIDDEN TREASURE: *THE MARK*

When a sign embedded in rock is recognised, it signifies import!

A WORD FROM THE WORD

אוֹת

aot – "sign"

But wait, surely this photograph has slipped into the series in error? The Roman Empire could not have emerged in the worst nightmare of the first family! The Pilgrim's Journal will record the entry of "a sign" into the digging for gems in Genesis. We shall be set to rights as the text becomes lucid, clear and plain.

A VIEWPOINT TO PONDER
How may a sign signifying death be a pointer to life?

One of the strangest anomalies of life and death is the ONE act of grace that brought about the redemption of humankind. What had entered into Eden was the grimy growth of sin that needed cleansing, eradication. It was achieved when *YHVH* stepped in!

Cain was in trouble. He had become a murderer. How could he explain his action to *YHVH*? *Am I my brother's keeper? Am I required to monitor his comings and goings?* Cain handled that interrogation feeling somewhat relieved. To his own mind, Cain had handled a dastardly situation rather well.

But when a further challenge impacted his brain, Cain hit rock bottom! The following question was enough to awaken Cain, too late, to his dastardly deed. *Where is your brother? His blood is crying out to Me from the ground!' Now you are in a worse condition than Abel and his blood which flowed from your hand.* Cain then realised what he had really done! The condition of his soul made itself plain and Cain repented sincerely, realising there would be consequences: *My punishment is more than I can bear for I will be driven from Your Presence.*

There is another significant matter to be dealt with here. *YHVH* had heard Cain's faintest cry! Because of his turn of mind and heart—his repentance—Cain would not receive the death penalty. *YHVH* would still make a way for Cain. How so? Cain was to live, marry, and receive a family. Here, the gem of grace. Wonderful! Grace is discovered before the Age of Grace.

And, if Adam and Eve were the only people on Planet Earth *in the beginning,* who, in the realms of reality, could Cain have married? Adam and Eve were the progenitors of the Hebrew people. In the "days" when God created the universe, "man"—*adam,* the male and female varieties—were created in abundance as were every other creature. For example, the race known as the Neanderthals, extant in Europe in palaeolithic times, left undeniable evidence of their existence.

The most valuable of all the gems thus far unearthed from Genesis is found in chapter 4:16. The English translation states that Cain received a **mark** to keep him from harm. The Hebrew rendition reveals the nature of that mark! The word which is our present focal point contains ת = *"t"* . Ancient Hebrew formed *"t"* thus: ✝. Cain's mark could be rendered: *salvation via the cross*!

HIDDEN TREASURE: *RENEWAL*

The worst of winter past makes way for blossomed spring.

A WORD FROM THE WORD

הרא

qara – "call"

Can winter "call" the spring"? We cannot determine the wonders of winter but, though we may wish for warmer days, the winter holds its splendours. The fall of snow, icicles holding fast to the branches, the respite from summer sun, and autumnal maturity, add to the blessings of the months that have "gone to sleep". The awakening is glorious! How magnificent the blossom that calls forth the leaves and fruit, opening the way to renewal!

A VIEWPOINT TO PONDER
How would nature "know" the turning of the months?

Perhaps it is the mighty "voice" of the sun, calling the Earth to obey its every command or, consider the unerring movement of Earth pursuing its annual course. However, the "call" is heard: the Earth continues on its unerring route to bring renewal.

PILGRIM'S JOURNAL: Genesis 4:25–26

The grieving parents were emerging from the "winter" of their sorrows. Two sons, disparate in character, yet each loved by Adam and Eve, were lost to them by that deadly attack spawned by jealousy–cum–envy–cum—hatred. Now Mother and her beloved Adam must reach out to a new season where the return of spring will offer them the "fruit" they so desired.

The new season, where hope was translated into the joy of fulfilment, was underscored by a baby's cry. Adam and Eve had heard the "call" of new life, new hope, and a new springtime.

Baby Seth needed, instinctively, the comfort of Mother's arms and, though he knew it not at the time, the security of his Father's watchful care. The "first family" were a family again, a family renewed. It was like winter ceding its stronghold to spring. A wonderful gift was given: the gem of **renewal**.

It was the time of new beginnings. Be it noted that, in the dialogue of prayer from Edenic days, *YHVH*—the LORD—had called upon Adam. He was the One who took the initiative when walking in the garden with His devoted man and, searching for His miscreant man in the wilderness. God called to those to whom He had granted that "knowledge beside knowledge"— the spirituality that enabled humanity to commune with Divinity. *Adam, where are you? Are you ready to listen to My word for you? My will for you? My way for you?*

How grief, regret, sorrow, can impact upon the desire to listen to the LORD, respond, and ask for the aid of the LORD. It is so often, at the very time when communion—that is, prayer—is most needed, that the meeting is abandoned.

Yet *YHVH* is never keen to abandon the meeting for prayer, for converse, communication, and the contracting of a pilgrim's aim to worship, and to walk, in the path of God's purposing.

The new spring turned, in time, to summer, and summer into the maturity of autumn. Then, in the fruitful days of fulfilment, **Seth learned to initiate the call**! (Genesis 4:26).

THE REFLECTIVE GLANCE

THE SEASONS OF LIFE MAY REACH DEEP INTO
THE SOUL AND EACH HAVE THEIR PART TO PLAY
IN THE FORMATION OF CHARACTER.

* WHERE IS FAITH?

Where is there found a vibrant faith
Within a weary land?
Not worthy of the grace of God
It's true, but we believe
His loving care we will receive:
A living faith will stand.

Where can be found an active faith
Within a pagan land?
When trust is energised by hope,
Eroding fears are gone:
'Just say the word, LORD, it is done,
Your word is my command.'

Where is there found a living faith
Within a grieving land?
Though shadows fall, He hears our call
And, in the grief of loss,
We find the Counsellor because
He takes our trembling hand.

There can be found a steadfast faith
Within a burdened land!
For, where the sorrows of the heart
By grace have been transformed,
A fragile faith will be reformed
And joy needs no demand!

It is in the plan of God that we should walk by faith and not by sight. Sight—the visual aid, the "Picture Parable"—was required in the earliest of humankind's progress through the "days" of creation (e.g. the "tree", the "snake"), but our capacity to walk by faith was encouraged by using our inner eyes: the mind, and soul. Seth had taken a new step toward maturity.

THE FORWARD GLANCE

THE REALISATION THAT GOD, WHO IS LORD OF THE UNIVERSE, TAKES AN INTEREST IN HUMAN JOYS, PAIN, ASPIRATIONS AND ABILITIES, IS AWE-INSPIRING.

* GOD'S STEADFAST LOVE

How steadfast is the love of God!
It does not change, it will abide;
God's loving-kindness does not cease,
We find in Him the heart's deep peace.

How constant is the grace of God,
Revealed within His precious word;
So undeserved, yet bountiful,
It is through grace we are made whole.

How faithful are the ways of God:
He keeps His word: He is the LORD!
His promises remain secure,
And through the ages will endure.

How lasting is our joy in God!
We walk by faith, we trust His word;
The LORD is our inheritance:
He is our hope, we're in His hands.

The endless love of God prevails,
His boundless mercy never fails;
It's new each morning! This our praise:
Great is His faithfulness always!

The onward march of humankind has gathered many truths through the study of God's word—the Bible—and by the "tutor" of experience. In both, we discover that the principles of life and living that were evident in Genesis have a resonance of truth that guides all who will set themselves to pilgrimage today! The gems unearthed in Genesis thus far have enriched the mind and soul of those on the journey of faith and, as we break new ground, astounding worth may be unearthed from every page!

HIDDEN TREASURE: *LINEAGE*

The soul should look to the right sentinel when seeking direction.

A WORD FROM THE WORD

אב

ab – "father", "ancestor"

This mountain marked the near environs of my childhood, island home. It was the sentinel, located at the head of the Huon Valley, Tasmania. All residents of the valley are able to sight their way home via the mount (though the highways have a decisive role to play). Mount "Sleeping Beauty" sheltered the valley from winter's raging storms. Ever "asleep", yet "Beauty" was clad appropriately each season—the glistening white of winter, the spritely welcoming hues of spring, the purple of summer, and the placid mauve of autumn. The seasons meld together to mark the years, aiding the march of a family's age.

A VIEWPOINT TO PONDER
How do genes confirm identity?

Genes prove family! If there is any doubt as to the identity of a wandering vagrant seeking a confirmation of a home address, the reading of the data specifies relationships. It's much the same as a fingerprint, in terms of precision. There is only one thumb-print like my thumb-print: mine! But I belong to "family"!

PILGRIM'S JOURNAL: Genesis 4:17–26

From the closing verses of Genesis 4, we enter a new phase of these unique records. The 1st generation has produced the 2nd, and the 3rd follows on. The family of humankind is expanding and the genealogies, the **lineage**, of the various personalities are tabulated in precise and intricate detail.

There are some precious gems about to be unearthed which have been hidden away in records long thought to be far too ancient to be of any modern consequence. First to surface is the Hebrew word for *father*. This name is far from being a formal appendage for the term is a name for home-life, warm and meaningful. אָב is best translated as "dad", or "daddy". However, in a tabulation such as that under scrutiny, the word may also carry the flavour of the *ancestry* of a given "clan".

The feasible connotation of ancestry provides a highly probable, if not definitive, reason for the given extremes attached to the length of a person's life in the early chapters of Genesis! Then, as the spade is taken to the name "father", it is quite remarkable to uncover another gem hidden away in the soil of Genesis. Go once more to page 158 and inquire as to what the most ancient form of the letters א and ב will uncover. Here are the "Picture Parables" for "father": *the predominant one is in the house, the home.* He is "at home" with his family!

To the amazement of us all, no doubt, Cain founded a city! One can but surmise that this would be a conglomeration of mud huts! Though, if we are reading the text in terms of ancestry, it could well mean the continuing family line of Cain. Some interesting details emerge as to the character of some!

In the family line of Seth, evidence of a continuance of a reverence for the LORD is on record. Therefore, it may be assumed that Seth, who stood on the mountain heights of the most ancient form of faith, encouraged that quality within his family for, with him, *people began to call on the Name: YHVH.* Enoch was such a man. His spirituality was noted, not only by his family members but by the LORD who *took him HOME.*

HIDDEN TREASURE: *MUSIC*

The sweetest melodies are those that enrich the soul.

A WORD FROM THE WORD

נגינה

neginah – "music"

Though I lived for a time in Scotland and love the distinctive sound of the bagpipes, my mother's heritage is Ireland and so it was that, when the family was seated around the home fire, our evenings were often filled with the melodious sounds of Ireland warming our hearts. Those songs enriched the young by filling our lungs, mind, and the soul, with stories set in song. It is no wonder that I retain those songs and sentiments!

A VIEWPOINT TO PONDER
Can a tune reach further into the soul than the words?

The tune is the vehicle by which the words sink themselves into the soul. It is the truth that must be retained. It is what counts.

PILGRIM'S JOURNAL: Genesis 4:21

I had to go searching for the appropriate gem when setting my mind to the Scriptural setting of **music**. Somewhat surprisingly, it took a search into Lamentations (the sorrows of Jeremiah, known as "the weeping prophet"), to find the appropriate word from which to extract the gem. The tears of people bowed down by the griefs occasioned by family disputes may indeed be the harbinger of a solemn strain: the Psalms abound in the solemn and, the joyful. They are meant to be chanted or, sung!

As for "A Word from The Word", *neginah* presents a letter not yet encountered. Found in the heart of the word is ג *gimel*—the camel! There is no need to go into a definitive explanation: the camel carries its burden through the valleys, and on into the arid country where the desert journey is alleviated by the faithfulness of this "special friend", the camel!

So, we will pick up the strains: Jabal and Jubal come to the fore: they are the sons of Lamech and Adah. Their names are so similar, they could have been twins. The boys pursued vastly different interests. Jabal herded cattle. Perhaps Jubal was fascinated by the music of birds and their song. But though he tried to mimic them, his pitch and key seemed inadequate.

Here is a possible scenario: Jubal, lounging by a pool, nonchalantly pulled a reed from the water, blew upon the reed. What a pleasing sound! He tried it again. Oh, but there is a slight hole in the reed. His finger covered it. The sound was changed. He placed more holes, testing the reed: thus, music was born.

With apologies to Julie, my song of praise:
Doh: The gift to make my bread, *(my sustenance)*
Ray: The sun upon my face *(Son-light: the best I know)*
Me: Recipient of grace *(undeserved but freely given)*
Fah: Outlasting time and space *(Eternity is in sight)*
Soh: I plan to walk God's paths *(The Bible is my Guide)*
Lah: The sound of heart-felt Psalms *(songs of the soul)*
Te: The sign that grants me life *(Consider an ancient †)*.
Dough has turned to "bread", my song to … joy!

HIDDEN TREASURE: *CHARACTER*

Trees, and people, that reach for the light will grow straight.

A WORD FROM THE WORD

הֲנוֹדְ

heno__ch__ – "Enoch"

To walk among tall timber is awe-inspiring. The canopy is high above but the pathway is plain for the sunlight filters through the ever-green eucalypts. To bring the further blessing, the leaves share the pungent aroma of their unique genre. For those sensitive to nature's gifts, tall timber grants rich lessons of life. Straight of limb is one thing, straight of character is more to be desired in growth, in usefulness—in the present and the future.

A VIEWPOINT TO PONDER
What may I learn from the growth of a tree?

How does one learn anything? It comes to mind that a teacher can only teach a subject when it is learned. When is a lesson really learned? When it is lived. Lived? Practise makes perfect!

PILGRIM'S JOURNAL: Genesis 5

Who could have believed it? There are two men by the name of Enoch in the earliest known genealogies of humankind! One was the son of Cain (Gen. 4:17), and the other was a man well down the line of Seth (Gen. 5:18). The names were identical, the meaning of each was likewise: Enoch means *teacher.*

Schooling in those far-off days was restricted to the home. Cain knew of no schools in the vicinity. Still, Cain had once been "schooled" in the home of his parents. Though, as we are well aware, Cain had been the recalcitrant bad-boy! But Cain had learned his lessons the hard way. Cain learned that there were consequences for bad behaviour. Those consequences could not have been more disastrous!

One can easily believe that the disciplines learned in the tent of Cain would have been more stringent than those laid down by his parents, Adam and Eve. When Cain and his wife named their first-born, it was their earnest desire, no doubt, that little baby Enoch would—in growing to manhood—become a teacher for the children he and his wife would raise.

Uncle Seth's descendant, Enoch, became a man whose name has been remembered through all-but countless centuries for a quite remarkable reason. First, an observation of the name, by which to draw out the gem: The ancient pictorial account of the Hebrew alphabet (page 158), is serving us well. Observe ה: the vision, נ: the tenacious, ו: the connected, and כ (in its final form) = ך: hands-on activity. Here would be a man of **character**!

What do we read for the teacher? A good teacher will provide viewpoints that lead to right answers for learning and living. The tenacious teacher will keep on keeping on in the face of immense difficulties. The best teacher is able to connect, to communicate with, his/her pupils. The final letter, the opened hand, marks the quality of being involved in the on-going teacher–learner link! Here is Enoch, the exemplary teacher because he was a man who walked with God! Enoch has much to teach us today. His life's inheritance remains: learn / teach well.

HIDDEN TREASURE: *THE GENERATIONS*

Even the most tender plant should find a place to grow.

A WORD FROM THE WORD

תּוֹלְדוֹת

toledoth – "generation"

The eucalypt ascends to the canopy of the forest. I was thrilled to find this tender shoot of the plant—the Blue Gum, Tasmania's state emblem—near the beginning of its life. Here is the re-birth of a tree! It has far to travel, upwards! As I come to think of it, this is how we too must travel: reaching up, ever up and, as we do so, our branches will reach out far and wide, though never separated from the trunk and the roots of the tree.

A POINT TO PONDER
What is to be said for a second birth?

There is no going back to the starting place! All depends on a change of heart. And no, not via surgery! It is a matter of the life of the soul and it requires a decision—a change of motive, of outlook, of attitude, of life-style, of heart. At the "heart" of us, a radical change takes place: our "heart-beat" is to the good, the ill is discarded. The New Life has begun!

PILGRIM'S JOURNAL: Genesis 5

Genesis, chapter 5 commences with the words, *this is the book of the generations of Adam. In the day that Adam was created, he was made in the likeness of God.*

Much had happened in the chronology of the times, places, and the characters of the succeeding **generations** of the Adamic line. We have been confronted with the good and the ill, the right and the wrong displayed in the lives of those who lived and died as generations passed from one to the other.

In Biblical terms, a generation does not necessarily mean the child of the father. Alternatively, we may be looking at key personnel listed for scrutiny in a family's lineage, or ancestry. Take the clan of Cain, for example. The matter of a re-birth is probable in his family line as we have already observed.

In seeking to determine the value of the gem unearthed in this present study, it is again helpful to observe the "Picture Parables" discovered in Ancient Hebrew (page 158)—*tav:* sign of the cross—*vav used as an o:* being held—*lamed:* the guide—*daleth:* access—another *vav (o):* held—2nd *tav (th):* the sign! If, in these latter days, we are able to acknowledge the fulness of meaning in the sign—the cross—salvation is our beginning and our ending! We are held in God's Hands, and we may use the door as our access to God or, conversely, our freedom to the world at large. The decision has always been ours to make.

It has been said: prayer is so simple. It is akin to walking through a doorway that "opens" into the Presence of God. Here we may make our petitions known whether by voice or by our prayer-thoughts. And, we may come to listen… to *listen!* The choice does not matter: just to be there, in God's Presence, IS prayer!

In giving a succinct answer to that question regarding the second birth, we have left much unsaid. What can be said now, however, by giving thought to prayer, we have disclosed the soul's source of sustenance. The soul finds its inner strength by absorbing the word of God—in its printed form and, in prayer.

HIDDEN TREASURE: *HERITAGE*

Aging "boughs" do not measure character but shelter gives peace

A WORD FROM THE WORD

מתושלה

methuselah – "Methuselah"

My father's blood-line is a lengthy one. His father did not reach old age. His father before him sailed to Port Arthur, Tasmania, from Oxford, England, under guard! News of the clan before his birth is rather scarce, though it is known he was a boatman on the Thames. When digging out the records, it was discovered that the ancestor entered England with the Normans. In long years prior to this event, the name was carried from the far north in Viking territory. There the Turfrey forebear was discovered. The family name was *Thorfrieda*–a gem: *God's Peace.*

A VIEWPOINT TO PONDER
Does a blood-line carry more than blood?

The blood-line carries "characteristics" though not character. The disciplines enjoined through "folk-lore" may guide to peace.

PILGRIM'S JOURNAL: Genesis 5:21–32

We now greet a man blessed with both the lengthiest of names and the length of his years! That's about all that is known of Methuselah. He is overshadowed by his father, largely because of the outstanding character displayed in the life of Enoch. It is to be expected, however, that something of the gracious, saintly character of Enoch would have so impressed his son, his many children, that they would have exercised a desire to emulate the goodness of their father. Methuselah drew on family **heritage**.

I find it possible to split Methuselah's name in half! There is *Methu…* Hmm, how about the worthy name *Matthew*—meaning *gift of Yahweh*—a gem! And, *Selah*—perhaps a term used in signalling a pause in later Temple chants for *pause, think on it*!

No mention of the character of Methuselah, however, is left on record in the lengthy charts of Genesis that tabulate a family line (and most infrequently, the family heritage). At the core of human character is the key factor disclosed in the days of creation as God said, *let Us make mankind in Our likeness.* It is possible to reflect the nature that is imparted by God! Look at Enoch. Where is a better example? And Methuselah—if indeed he is the pro-genitor of Matthew: *the gift of YHVH.*

We come late to a description of the tree and what it can represent in terms of the "Picture Parable". A sensitive observation notes the tree "reaching down" to lift the branch, emulating a parent's love. It has taken many years for that trunk to develop, the branches to finally fall due to the weight of the wood! In accord with the nature of its genre, the branches have spread out every which-way! And, is not this the nature of the off-spring of any well-formed family—to move off every which-way as they pursue their individual hopes and aspirations?

The aspect most notable about this tree is the spritely sprigs just forming at the extremities of the twigs. And, above all, the health of the foliage. The leaves tell the story of the tree: here is *Life!* What is the gauge of our health, yours and mine—the "leaves", the quality of years already spent or, invested?

HIDDEN TREASURE: *GRACE*

A sentinel stands in the sun but broken lives cling to the shadows.

A WORD FROM THE WORD

חן   מצא   נח

chen – "Grace"   *matsa* – "found"   *no'ch* – "Noah"

That an erstwhile trader in human slaves could find it in his soul to pen the words of what has become one of the best-loved hymns of all time—*Amazing Grace*—can mean nothing short of the miracle of which he writes. After experiencing a life-or-death experience in the throes of a devastatingly furious gale, John Newton discovered that his plea for mercy gifted him with something better! Newton was transformed. He found GRACE!

A VIEWPOINT TO PONDER
What can I do to obtain grace?

Do? There is no deed, no action, no "payment" by which grace may be obtained. Just ask for it in faith. A free gift, grace is granted to those who don't deserve it, but who accept it by faith!

PILGRIM'S JOURNAL: Genesis 6:1–8

What is it about grace that is so "amazing"? Newton found it so for, at the tiller of his slave ship about to founder in the raging waves with the loss of all personnel—bond and free—he found himself in the extremity of life. Newton was forced, in the wind and the waves, to finally see himself for the crude, heartless travesty of humanity that he was. Newton needed help. Facing the fury of the gale, Newton now came face-to-face with reality. "Oh God, I need help!"

Newton later testified, as a man reborn, about the result of his dramatic change of heart: **Grace**… *saved a wretch like me… I once was lost… blind… I could not see… and grace my fears relieved… How precious was that grace… (*from*) the hour I first believed…* John Newton gave his life from thence to aid suffering humanity and was able to testify that he knew he was not what he ought to be, not what he wanted to be, but by the grace of God: *I am what I am!*

Amazing grace has led us to the son of Lamech. Lamech is featured in Scripture only because his claim to fame is through the men who were his forebears and, in turn, his son! Genesis 5:25 – 31 outlines what we do know of Lamech. Methuselah was his father—there were enough years and to spare for Lamech to gather the values revealed in the life of his father, reputed to be the oldest person in history!

Lamech must have needed comforting for he named his new-born son Noah which sounds like the Hebrew for *comfort*. Somehow, Lamech must have steered Noah in the right direction for his son *found* **grace** *in the eyes of the YHVH– LORD!* Lamech is remembered, also, for his attitude to everything about him. It all existed under a cloud and that cloud was God's doing! Where is the gem? And, what is its worth?

One of the great wonders of Genesis is that grace is found anywhere for those willing to use a spade to find the gem—the "ruby", of course, for a cross would one day be stained in Blood as Jesus stepped in to right the wrongs of sin though grace.

HIDDEN TREASURE: *COVENANT*

Trees growing in accord with their planting confirm a straight path.

A WORD FROM THE WORD

ברית
berith – "covenant"

Melbourne has been termed a "Garden City" and with good reason! Its suburbs abound in trees in a multitude of varieties. The evergreens are balanced by deciduous glory in autumn. The streets are lined, and gardens make a home for many more. The tree, if it could speak, would no doubt thank the gardener for choosing it and tending it through the years. And, we–the gardeners–have "covenanted" with the tree to ensure its continued well-being. My apple tree, also the pencil pine, have lost a branch recently. Have I failed in my duty of care?

A VIEWPOINT TO PONDER
What more than the spade and the spray must I utilise?

Oh yes, the ground must be tended and the tree kept clean, but the tree requires nurturing, some food, and training on the way.

Oh, to walk an avenue in winter (with a scarf and gloves of course), realising that a brisk breeze warns of impending storms. Spring allows the savouring of newness of life all about. The trees grant relief from blatant summer sun. And, I rejoice in the colours splashed all about that whisper autumn in the wind.

The seasons hold their promises and it is this word that introduces us to one of the richest of all gems hidden away in Genesis. The promise in question has a special name which must be investigated as this trek through the introductory book opens to view the astounding truths to be housed in the Bible. This gem will now be taken in hand. It is the **covenant**.

What is a covenant? Like an avenue, it consists of two sides and carries a special connotation—depending on who are the participants in that covenantal promising. Basically, there are also two kinds of covenants: that made between equals, friends, strangers, or those wishing to seal a deal, ensuring the ratification of the promise. The second type of covenant is that made between unequals, e.g., a king and a vassal. What the vassal was unable to do was to match the promise of the king. The vassal would agree to abide by the terms of the covenant.

The covenants that the LORD has made with humanity stretch from Genesis to Revelation and reach on down into today's frenetic circumstance, challenging the very soul of us! And, it goes without saying that God keeps His promises! On the other hand, humanity has tended to fail to keep any one of those promises! We will meet up with this gem again!

The first evidence of covenant-making is recorded in Genesis 6:18. *YHVH* has declared His intention to flood the Earth. Why was Noah selected to undertake this enterprise of ensuring the continuance of life in the face of the catastrophe? *Noah was a righteous man and walked with God… And Noah did everything according to the request of God* (vs. 9, 22). The LORD recognises righteous living and will enter into Covenant with all who are prepared to take Him at His word, obey His known will.

HIDDEN TREASURE: *THE PROMISE*

A well-built vessel can weather the fiercest of life's storms.

A WORD FROM THE WORD

המבּוּל
hamabbul – "The Flood"

A famous archaeologist, Sir Leonard Woolley, his wife and a colleague were excavating near the coastline of the southern end of the Black Sea in search of ancient artifacts. Much was found and then the team met what appeared to be the base of civilisation. Ignoring the urge to conclude the dig, it was continued deep into the sedimentary sand. Near four metres was lifted. "That's it. Finished!" "No,' replied Woolley, "Let's keep on." Suddenly, there it was, an artefact far more ancient than anything yet unearthed. "What have we here?" His wife replied, 'We have found "The flood!"'

A VIEWPOINT TO PONDER
Can we assume that The Flood was a global event?

Legend would be adamant. The Bible says so! When the actual records were set down, the world view had no conception of a globe. The world Noah knew was confined to a limited expanse.

Many have been the suggestions, and the assertions, as to the nature and extent of what is known as "The Deluge". What we tend to leave "on the back burner" is the reason why The Flood occurred. Genesis 6 paints a gruesome picture, succinct but adamant. How soon humanity fell from its lofty heights in terms of the quality of character which was the natural outflow of human aspirations that sought to follow the known will of *YHVH*–LORD.

There is a school of opinion that, at the end of the Ice Age, the melting glaciers flowed on down through Europe into the Mediterranean Sea with the water levels rising dramatically as an inevitable consequence. The remarkable topography of the Bosporus was such that the rising sea gushed into the Black Sea at a catastrophic rate, the rush of water becoming many, many times that of Niagara Falls (see the previous page).

The world of Noah and the known civilisation in that world of what now could be termed "The Middle East" was facing the end! There is also substantive evidence of a deluge of like proportions in Mesopotamian records. Both Hebrew Scripture and cuneiform data are supportive of The Deluge.

The traditional approach must be treated with utmost respect. Yes, "the world" was inundated. All known life was destroyed. The Biblical scribe had no news of any such occurrence in e.g., USA or Australia, but extant data is supportive! Where does this pilgrim stand? It is acknowledged that Noah's world was a "small" world. His world was destroyed. Archaeology attests to the inundation. And, the new world that emerged following the end of The Deluge is a documented fact!

Finally, the clouds rolled back to allow the sun to shine once more. Sun on retreating showers: light is allowed its full display as it expressed the **Promise** of God. "Here is the planet I have gifted you. Never again a flood such as that one! Here is the promise: red of Blood, orange warmth of kindness, gold of Grace, green of Life, blue of Holiness, purple of The Kingdom!"

A Gem – Noah

THE SAILOR

See now this ship—this ark—
how sure, secure, its rugged frame.
The cubits and the shape
are right. The finished work,
I see it now: it is a ship, an ark,
a style of form beyond
men's strangest dreams.

One thing:
How did God know that I'd obey?
He tested faith, it seems!

See now these many beasts:
from east and west they come
in pairs for sheltering within
this solid, wooden ark.
See how they hasten here.

One thing:
How will I tend this stock?
By patient calm, it seems.

See now this looming mist,
this nimbus cloud grows bold
to pierce the peerless blue
and threaten all the land.
The heav'ns will weep today!

One thing:
how did He shut us in?
It is by grace, it seems.

Where is the night, the day?
Who knows? Ha! Nature knows
her times by crowing cock!

NOAH

One thing:
How will we know the opening day?
It is by trust, it seems!

See how this gentle dove,
this pleasant dove, has brought
to us the news of unabated flood.
She found no place to rest,
to nest, upon the seething, the
tempestuous, raging sea.
(The raven now is lost to us).

One thing:
Who knows the way to land?
God steers us on, it seems.

See now, I wait…
At evening hour, my dove,
how does she fare, out there?
Will she return? Oh, yes,
my dove! "Peace" brings
an olive-leaf!

One thing:
When will we find the sun again?
In God's own time, it seems.

The dawn has come,
the mountain height is dry!
This ark of grace is open wide
and stock, redeemed, emerge
to face a new and sunlit day.

One thing… O LORD,
what awesome sight is this,
where splendid colours lay?
It is Your Promise Bow: I see!

HIDDEN TREASURE: *REST*

A vacant chair may spell grief for the past but hope for the future.

A WORD FROM THE WORD

יוֹנָה
Yonah – "dove"

The dove was free! The tempest had subsided. I woke to a raging tempest this morning. Here it is, summer time! Why should I feel this icy blast of wind and weather when the sun should be sending its zenith smile? The media proclaims the onslaught of climate change, though some brave souls will point to global warming. There are consequences for a disrespect of Earth's daily gifts. Nature cannot stand so much carelessness.

A VIEWPOINT TO PONDER
How is it possible that a rainbow can form a bow?

The rainbow is one of nature's wonders. It needs the rain but, mainly, when it is past. Then, the sun. The bow is a miracle!

The LORD signs His promises! There was a signal in the sky to sign off on His great declaration that the Earth would never again see such a devastating result of humankind's utter rejection of all the Creator had placed in its hands.

The scene opens a "Picture Parable" to view. It will illustrate the after-math of the global catastrophe occasioned by "The Flood" and has much to say which should find an echo in our heart-felt thanksgiving. The top of the mountain is seen through the mist; the sea is calm; the boat is at **rest**. The trees have reclaimed their territory; the sun is gifting its light to the passing storm. But, where is life? the scene is empty! There is much that is pleading for renewal as Noah takes stock of everything.

There is a hidden gem that is related to the rainbow! Thoughtful people, still attributing the phenomenon to God's promising (which always stands the test of time!), are aware that the rainbow will reveal its miraculous bow upon the cloud after the storm has passed. It then allows the sun its variegated "paintbrush" to complete the picture.

However, it is not only afterwards that a rainbow can be seen for it will depend upon the current location of the sun! The rainbow tells a vastly different story in the morning! The sun is then given to shining on the approaching storm before it occurs. What, then, could be the ramifications of nature's bow when the sun is shining upon the clouds in the morning? The bow is informing us that there is a storm approaching! Take your umbrella!

The LORD is always pleased when He is able to declare that the "storm" is now past. However, He is not backward in coming forward when there is a necessity of issuing a warning as to an impending "storm". His warning is always in time for humankind to take stock of the situation and to take remedial action by being prepared to face all that life can throw at us. And, after the "storm" has passed, to find rest for the soul! What a gift, a gem, for those who can "read God's writing" on daily events!

HIDDEN TREASURE: *THE MOUNTAIN*

"Diablerets", *Devil's Mountain"*, has been conquered!

A WORD FROM THE WORD

הר
har – "mountain"

It was a glorious day. Summer at its best. Not a breeze stirred. As I stood near the summit of this Swiss mountain, I was in awe, not only of the superior mountain views abounding in Switzerland, but also the message conveyed by the cross that surmounted the rugged peak. Indeed, this mountain bears the ignominious title of *Diablerets.* But this mountain does not belong to Satan. Perhaps the unfortunate title stemmed from the nature of the climb! I had taken the easy way: the cable car! There are mountains that cannot be conquered except by extreme exertion. Mountains of the spiritual kind require faith.

A POINT TO PONDER
Faith? Small as a mustard seed, like mine? Sufficient?

That is what Jesus said. and, He ought to know. He was to climb the most massive of all peaks with the heaviest burden!

PILGRIM'S JOURNAL: Genesis 9

The world of Noah and his family was emerging from unprecedented depths of water. They stood, at last, on dry ground: on the **mountain** top. Their sense of awe in what lay behind them in terms of the catastrophe, and what lay ahead of them in terms of hope, opened into worship of the LORD. Here, a sense of sacrifice was being ratified: here heartfelt thankfulness was expressed.

One is reminded of King David, as he stood at last, on a strategic mountain-top at the moment when he secured the ground on which Jerusalem would be built. Araunah, the Jebusite, freely offered the summit of the mountain into David's keeping. Then the king declared: *I will never offer to the LORD that which costs me nothing!* (2 Samuel 24:16–24).

For some, there may be no unique "mountain-top" experiences but, in the visionary moments of many, there is a moment in time when one is confronted with a life-changing event. Such a moment would be that when—at a time when the presence of God is made paramount in worship—there is the ready response of an entrance into covenant.

Many are the occasions when the upward climb demands the exertion of energy that requires the utmost input to the venture. When I was visiting Yosemite National Park, USA, with friends, someone pointed to a climber, high on the cliff of the façade of El Capitan, the sheer cliff located near the entrance to the Park. "He has been climbing that cliff for three days, non-stop!" I was impressed! The cliff faces which challenge even the most intrepid traveller can be most daunting. Hold to the "rope"!

The descent from a mountain-top experience is seldom mentioned but can be far more daunting! Just ask Noah! What did he and his family carry? Some commodities relate to the physical stamina acquired, and the mental tenacity honed by a positive outlook on life. They carried something else: they had each been gifted with, and carried with them, a spirituality trained by CONSCIENCE!

THE REFLECTIVE GLANCE

HOW CAN IT BE THAT, HAVING BEEN
GIFTED WITH THE ABILITY—VIA CONSCIENCE—
TO DISCERN THE RIGHT FROM WRONG, HUMANKIND SO
OFTEN DISREGARDS GOODNESS AND GRACE?
WHAT IS GOD'S ANSWER TO THE RIFT?

* IN TIMES GONE BY

In times gone by, the LORD declared
His word through prophets once inspired;
Down through the years, in various ways,
His voice was clear, His will desired.

There came a day, in God's own time,
When He redeemed us through His Son;
Jesus, Creator, Heir of all,
By Him the darkest night is gone!

Sustaining all things by His word,
He came to make us whole, and clean!
He sits enthroned, the Lord of Life,
Beside the Majesty of Heaven.

His throne will last forever and
His royal sceptre will defend;
He rules by grace in righteousness,
His tide of years will never end.

God's Answer for human sin reaches out from Eternity and, because Jesus—the Christ, the Promised One—is eternal, it is right to introduce Him for He was *In the Beginning ...*

John sets the matter right in his matchless Prologue (John1;1-14): **In the beginning** *was The Word and He was with God for He was—and IS—God! Everything in existence was made by Him. In Him was—IS—the source of Life. The Life He imparts brings light (enlightenment), to humanity. This Light shines through the darkness and the darkness will never obliterate the Light!*

You wish to discover what God—*YHVH*—is like? See Him in the Face of Jesus. His Light is "Rainbow" Light!

THE FORWARD GLANCE

SOMETIMES A SONG CAN SAY IT BEST,
THE MUSIC BEING THE VEHICLE WHICH CARRIES
THE TRUTH OF THE GOSPEL FROM THE PAGE
INTO HUMAN MINDS AND HEARTS.

* WORLD VALUES
Tune: *Saved by Grace*   D.L.M.

The peoples of the Earth can find
Faint hope on which to build their life;
The values of the world conspire,
Enclosing minds in earthly strife.
Oh Lord, we pray that light may shine
Into the darkness of the soul;
Lord, come, transform despair to joy,
O cast out care and make us whole.

The nations, in their restlessness
To gain life's best through selfish greed,
Neglect the virtues of Your word
And find no guide Your law to heed.
Lord, come into our troubled world
Where hate displaces human good;
Equip Your messengers with grace
That, by their lives, the Christ is heard.

Our world's adrift from what You planned
By colour, clime, by class and creed;
Though light still shines upon Your word,
The world prefers the darkest deed.
Lord, we would pray for every land;
Turn all our darkness into light,
Disperse the clouds of graft and greed
That, in our world, peace comes to sight!

Many gems have already been unearthed in Genesis as the spade has brought hidden treasure to light. Sometimes, even the enlightened need to be reminded of the responsibility we carry to share the Light which leads through night into DAY!

HIDDEN TREASURE: *BROTHERS*

When seeking adventure, it is circumspect to carry a guide book.

A WORD FROM THE WORD

בֵּן   אָח

ben – "son"   *a<u>ch</u>* – "brother"

The road leading on towards the purple peaked mountains of the Flinders Ranges is a road less traversed than any leading into a metropolis. Yet all roads make known their purpose. They will lead somewhere. All travellers—the tourist and the pilgrim—will take the highway that leads to the desired destination. Some will go further afield and seek another map to guide them. My brothers pursued their chosen paths but it was their sons who scattered further afield on the global map. The way ahead will sometimes daunt, sometimes elate, but all times will add to the wealth or otherwise of what the experience provides.

A VIEWPOINT TO PONDER
Is it more prudent to remain in the home environs?

Two of the great pilgrims of Biblical times were called to dissimilar locations: Abraham was called to launch out not knowing where he was going. Jeremiah was required to stay put. Both fulfilled their calling. Listen to the impulse of the soul.

The world was beckoning. It was time to depart the home tents. Noah had fallen into a drunken stupor—to the extent that one of his sons ridiculed his dad, while the other two carefully covered father's "shame". Blessings and a curse followed. And now, a careful consideration of the three sons, **brothers**, will send them on their way:

Shem: *Renown.* He was the first born. He was thought to be dusky. His descendants are said to have ranged from Elam—Mesopotamia—in the East, to the Mediterranean in the West. It is of interest here to note that the name "Shem" is the same as the Hebrew word for *name* but of greater import is that his son was named Eber: *a shoot*, the forebear of the *Hebrew* nation.

Japheth: *Extender, to widen.* It is said that Japheth could have been fair skinned and that he was probably the forebear of the Greeks and Romans. Also, there is a startling inclusion in the listings under his name: Magog means *high* and is thought to refer to the people of the north—the fair skin tends to agree with this. The news from Genesis 9:27 indicates that, because Japheth was enabled to "dwell in the tents of Shem" meant that he could share in the spiritual privileges of Shem.

Ham: *Crooked.* Ham was reputed to be dark skinned—some say, black. The probable route of Ham is said to have been Egypt, Cush, and Ethiopia. Others are of the opinion that Ham's descendants became the people of Canaan, a nation then marked by low morals and of corrupted behaviour.

Something further should be stated concerning the line of Shem which retained a strong religious base. It was to become the line from whom God gifted the world's Redeemer for Shem's descendants became the Israelites—the Jews! As Japheth's descendants were enabled to "dwell in the tents of Shem", sharing in the blessings of Shem, many would become faithful to God. Christians today share in that same blessing! The Jewish Baby, born in Bethlehem, has granted to all the greatest of gems: redemption through His Blood shed on Calvary!

HIDDEN TREASURE: *COMMUNITY*

Faulty components will not result in longevity, in bricks or humanity!

A WORD FROM THE WORD

שפה   אחד

shaphar – "language"   e*chad* – "one"

To have stood in the ruins, at the very centre of the arena of the Roman Colosseum, brought a solemnity of thought in the realisation that here, among others, Christians had faced the lions—martyrs for the faith they held. Blood had flowed on that ground, spawned by a hatred of alien concepts and, perhaps, a fear of what was represented in their faith. Could that fledgeling group gather strength to conquer the mighty Roman Empire? That ancient empire finally crashed. All who seek to rise should be sure that the ground on which they stand is stable and, true!

A VIEWPOINT TO PONDER
Will modern means of communication aid "community"

Via modern means, the world becomes localised! However, the younger generations need to recognise the dangers of, e.g., the mobile phone, as eye-to-eye contact fades from view!

Any gem to be extracted from Genesis 11 must be lifted early as the literature suddenly takes a down-hill journey, fast. A sense of unity prevails. Here is **community**. Community speaks of connection. Life was easy. All were of one mind, aims solidified. All spoke the same language! What could go wrong?

Community is not an easy goal to reach as the globe becomes localised. Still, modern society sets itself to achieve a like goal to that of Babel. Humanity's modern aspirations would have us reaching for the goal of UTOPIA!

Modern towers abound, set firm—seemingly—on the solid rock of "know-how" as the frame-work of steel and concrete, though clad in the fragile façade of glass, reach up to the sky. But how solid are the foundations of our highest ambitions? Would we climb the stairs of Modern Babel. Look first to the foundations:

$$\backslash\backslash | / / \qquad !$$

UTOPIA *Armageddon...*
1 WORLD RULE *$$$$$$$$$$ooo ... ...*
ALL WORLD TRADE Everyone *must comply...*
THE GLOBAL VILLAGE *Poverty, Poor, Pollution...*
WORLD IS CONQUERED *The Poor are subjugated...*
THE WORLD IS REACHABLE The Gospel reaches world!
NEWS: OUR WORLD A GLOBE The Church proclaims Truth

How soon Babel could change to "babble": *BABBLEON.* Incidentally, the location set down as *Shinar* was—in a later civilisation—renamed *Babylon.* Indeed, Babylon would become a mighty empire (known as the greatest, the empire of gold according to Nebuchadnezzar's dream—Daniel 2:29-35).

If the gem is to be accessed, its worth proved, how is the Community of Faith—The Church: **AT-ONE** in the soul—to ensure that the world we know today does not fall into decay? It may crash into the dust of Earth's, all too often, sordid history!

Check the foundations. Assess the framework. Choose durable cladding. Furnish the community with kindness. Welcome ALL!

HIDDEN TREASURE: *SCATTERED*

When natural elements are fractured, how does one build bridges?

A WORD FROM THE WORD

פוּץ

put̲s̲ – "scatter"

Often, when walking in my neighbourhood, I would encounter an Asian woman who showed no interest in my frequent nods, greetings, smiles. As Christmas loomed, I felt the barrier should be broken! I spoke. No response. I stepped into her path, took her arms, and extended my greeting. I received a responsive smile but discovered that she knew no English. Then, turning the corner into my street, I heard hurrying footsteps. I turned. It was the Asian who stepped into my path, lifted her arm, raised her thumb, and said everything necessary: "You O.K."

A VIEWPOINT TO PONDER
Why do so many aliens alienate?

Have you ever considered that, to a so-called alien, you may be the alien? What is an alien—any who have been refused "entry" into your environment? Build the bridge! Find words and deeds.

PILGRIM'S JOURNAL: Genesis 11:27–32

The thought has already been entered into this journal that one key reason for barriers to be erected against aliens is the fear of what they may introduce into one's frame of reference. Be it said and emphasised: aliens do not "pollute" the arena that I would claim as my own—I may be in fact the one who pollutes!

One way of dispatching fear of the unknown is to set about building bridges where the "flow of traffic" becomes desired, aliens become associates, strangers become known, and neighbours become friends.

What are the building blocks (must change that word: it can introduce the concept of barriers). Brick-work, that is better! And, more to the point, the bricks require a proficient mortar. The bricks? Actions carved by effort. The mortar? The adhesive of kindness will hold any two "bricks" together!

The arches will require specialised adaptation—that of being able to step over the non-essential issues so that a vision of the future may eventuate. The arch requires re-enforcement on both sides. This spells partnering, a vital aspect in the construction of the bridge. The bridge-builders—personnel determined to close the gap—will ensure the forming of lasting friendships and co-operative endeavours aimed at making Earth a better place in which to live and, dwell in peace.

The base which bonds the upright to the highway is the realisation that—when "bridges" are mended—the aliens are actually "family"! The **scattering** of humanity has enabled encounters that lead to unity! Here is the unearthing of the gem.

What appeared to the descendants of Noah to be another disaster, was—in actuality—the means whereby the LORD was allowing the Earth to receive the nurturing that had been neglected in humanity's bid to build a tower that would reach the sky without God's aid. The LORD had now set up a new way, a new opportunity to fulfil the aim, the purpose, of the covenanters to work in harmony with one another and with Him. When harmony is achieved, a symphony of community is reached!

HIDDEN TREAURE: *BLESSING*

A "bridge" can heal the barriers between East and West.

A WORD FROM THE WORD

ברכה
berakah – "blessing"

It was the eve of an international conference and, as a delegate, I was engaged in the registration process. I met with a young friend who would later become one of my students in Melbourne and, in later years, my near neighbour. Suddenly a pair of arms encircled my waist from the rear. I looked down to discover that those arms were black! Pure, shining black. I turned to find who was the source of the "embrace". It was an African who had been a delegate to a study course at which I had been the dean. He knew me well enough to know that he could surprise me with his greeting! We laughed, hugged and chatted!

A VIEWPOINT TO PONDER
Why is it that colour becomes such a barrier to unity?

When a surgeon calls for a blood transfusion for his patient, he does not request information concerning the donor's nationality! We are all "ONE" under the skin: ignorance is a major cause.

PILGRIM'S JOURNAL: Genesis 12:1–9

One would think that a scattering could never bring about a **blessing**, but the impossible can be possible. Certainly, one must dig deep beneath the alluvial soil of our trek to catch a glimpse of what may be termed a blessing in an alien culture!

From the deep south of Tasmania, to the far north of the globe, was indeed a scattering which took much grace to leave all, it seemed, that was conducive to happiness. I was to launch into the deep—well, not exactly—take flight, is a better description of the journey which found me, eventually in Russia.

I must affirm, however, that there were blessings in abundance: Misha, who gave aid in my move to a new residence; Alex—a very little boy—who offered his help; the man in the market, encouraging: "you are very welcome here." Then there was Maya, my main translator, who—after a morning session on Biblical content—came to me with the news: "I already had a knowledge of God in my head, but now I have Him in my heart." When a drastic illness necessitated an abrupt departure from Russia, another translator came to me with the most blessed news: "You turned the light on in my life." And, as I was about to depart, the customs official at Moscow Airport said, when looking at my passport: "You came to Russia to help our people. Thank you." What a beautiful epilogue. Blessings can abound at the most unexpected times and places!

The above lengthy introduction becomes this pilgrim's acknowledgement of how a scattering can enrich the life by the discovery of an unexpected gem! We have now entered a new phase in the saga of the generations who finally left home-soil to reach out into a world made new by the "Picture Parable" of a rainbow marking the end of The Deluge. Also, we can confirm the beginning of a covenantal relationship that would bring the glow of a gem discovered as Abram—cum—Abraham emerges on to the world scene.

While Abram was clearly of the blood line of Noah, he was to become known as "THE FATHER OF THE FAITHFUL"

HIDDEN TREASURE: *FELLOWSHIP*

The "ship of the desert" is a traveller's friend in arid lands.

A WORD FROM THE WORD

יחד
yachad – "together"

It takes some expertise to ride a camel. It was morning. On Mount Olivet, the camel—and his assistant (!)—were interested in accommodating me for a ride along the summit. Though the walls of the Old City of Jerusalem in the near vicinity beckoned me, what could be more inviting than an adventure on a "ship of the desert"? Accepting the offer, I found a reasonable amount of comfort—after surviving the mounting exercise! Then all went well until it was time to descend from said beast. It happened quickly! I slid, in a most ungainly way, down the neck of the camel as it knelt to rid itself of its burden! I'm sure the camel grinned as I stood again to dust myself and check my bones!

A VIEWPOINT TO PONDER
Be serious, what is the worth of a ship in the desert?

Nil, if one is searching for water! A ship is the vehicle that takes us to our desired goal. What is your goal? Choose the right ship!

PILGRIM'S JOURNAL: Genesis 12:1–9

Again, we are confronted with a genealogy peppered by names of men that also became the names of ancient cities. Many Bibles contain, before closing the back cover, a series of maps. The journey under scrutiny now is the first in the series.

Starting point: Ur of the Chaldeans is near to the north of the region known as the Fertile Crescent and in the northern area of what is known now as Mesopotamia. This region is situated mainly between the Euphrates and Tigris Rivers where the Babylonians dwelt. To the east of their homeland, was the ancient city of Nineveh. Abram—at the centre of our investigations—was the member of a family that adhered to the desires of their patriarch. Terah was the one who held the reins of this family and his word was the unwritten law of the clan!

It is thought that the initial impetus was to head for Canaan but the incentive was curtailed for, by the time the travellers reached Haran, Terah (the father of Abram, Nahor, and Haran) died. It is pertinent to note that the city of Haran—surely named in his honour—is extant today.

Route taken: the travellers made their way due west, following nature's compass points. Their most appropriate course would have been along the northern regions of the Fertile Crescent. Therefore, the "ship of the desert" would have had no extensive need to fill its hump with the elixir if life—water—beyond the norm. As they undoubtedly camped at the end of each day's trekking, these ancient pilgrims would have found adequate sustenance though of humble fare, for the onward journey.

The travellers, obviously, were a close-knit family group but their extensive journeying through unknown and, at times threatening, terrain, would have brought challenges to the camaraderie of their **fellowship**—and here is the gem! Many were the stories shared around the campfire and assessments made of their plans. So, in the face of the unknown, the family prayed together, stayed together, walked together and survived together. They had a clearly defined goal and adhered to it.

HIDDEN TREASURE: *FAITH*

It is possible to flourish in the desert if the Source of Life is found.

A WORD FROM THE WORD

ראה
raah – "cause to see"

It is a most remarkable experience, when least expected, as one negotiates the most arid territory—just pebbles atop the dry, red dust—the celebrated Sturt's Desert Pea reaching out across the ground. As the elongated shadows attest, it was yet early morning—an appropriate time to escape the harshest rays of summer sun! It is a joy just to remember the moment. What does the pea suggest? There is water nearby: faith soars!

A VIEWPOINT TO PONDER
Why do people decide to traverse the desert in summer?

It includes the call to duty, a restricted time span for the annual vacation, a vocational requirement, a necessity to reach a goal.

Where to from here? Terah was dead. Nahor and Haran had already agreed to settle in their new abode. The weather was more conducive to comfortable living conditions. There was ready access to the fundamental necessities of life. Why face an inhospitable desert? No, they were staying put.

What of Abram? Here's where the Biblical narrative marks a most strategic chapter in his life! The Voice of God would not be unknown to Abram while dwelling in Ur of the Chaldeans. He would have been aware of his family's ancient history. The situation has undergone a dramatic change however, and Abram has to now face new challenges.

Abraham has heard the unmistakable voice of *YHVH*: *Leave your country… your people… your father's household… Go to the land I will show you… I will make of you a great nation… I will bless you… I will make your name great… I will care for those who take care of you… Those who abuse you will be punished… And, every nation of Earth will be blessed because of you* (Gen.12:1–3). It was enough! Abram packed his bags.

Abram, the man who was to become Abraham and, as already noted, known as "The Father of the Faithful", is now revered in three major religions: Judaism, Christianity, and Islam.

It is timely to consider the nature of faith. What is **faith**? It has been best expressed to me by a friend whom I visited not long before her early death. At the time of our last meeting, Barbara was paralysed, with the only movement possible being with her head! We spoke together about our faith journey and I had the temerity to ask her how she would best describe faith. Barbara looked steadily at me, then said: *Faith is to put your hand out into the darkness, knowing it will be held!* Barbara had walked by faith many years: her ministry was blessed by God.

It is good to take cognisance of the three steps of faith:
1. I believe I can do it. 2. By faith I see 3. By trust I will succeed!
1. is thought; 2. is heart-felt, 3. is to act in faith—*this is a gem!*

HIDDEN TREASURE: *FAITHFULNESS*

When two are of like mind, they can reach a unified goal.

A WORD FROM THE WORD

שָׂרַי

sarai – "YHVH is prince"

Swans are remarkable birds for, after mating, they remain in a monogamous relationship throughout their lives. Their young are known as cygnets—which is where I first encountered such elegant and graceful birds for I taught, one day each week, at the Cygnet Area School as the itinerant art teacher. It was not far from my family home and it was always a delight to travel close by the mighty Huon River where the swans' movements were noted with pleasure. Here were "families" enjoying their placid marine environment, far from desert country.

A VIEWPOINT TO PONDER
If birds can stay together, why can't so many humans?

Birds, no doubt, live closer to the nature of their species. It takes love, but also a deep sense of faithful and monogamous commitment for men and women to control the straying eye syndrome. And, to make the right decision in the first place!!!

PILGRIM'S JOURNAL: Genesis 12:1–9

A major contributor to the monumentally important records of the life and times of Abram—Abraham—has already loomed large (though hidden to most), in the narrative. Here is a gem in the on-going story of the man of faith, Abram. Let me introduce you to the woman whose **faithfulness** strengthened Abram throughout his journeying. Here is Sarai (who would become known later as Sarah). Here is a precious gem indeed!

If Abram—Abraham—is to be known as the man of faith, it must be said that here is the one who displays a faithfulness worth lifting from beneath the alluvial ground of Genesis. Sarai was prepared to journey with her husband and his family. Sarai set out with eager anticipation to tread the same soil, encounter the same challenges, dream the same dreams, as her dearly beloved husband. Yes, Sarai could withstand the same rigours encountered by the men—all the way to their chosen goal.

The new home in what is now the city of Haran, was so delightful. It was wonderful to feel "at home" again! Sarai was tired. Now she was glad to ease her aching feet! And, it must be said, Sarai also held her private grief. Sarai remained childless. Perhaps, now that the journeying was finished, yes—perhaps—her highest hope would be fulfilled.

Then, Abram came to her with some very startling, and disconcerting news. He had received a special Calling from *YHVH.* "Dear heart, I have been asked to leave this place, leave my people, and go to a land that He will show me, He will guide me. I must obey. But, my dearest, I need you at my side. Will you come with me?" Pilgrims know the answer Abram received that night. The man of faith would be blessed by his beloved's faithfulness, Sarai would be ever at his side.

How surprising: Abram and Sarai's nephew, a lad by the name of Lot, became excited with the thought of a further expedition. He elected to join the pilgrims. But would Lot ever become a true pilgrim, or would he remain a tourist forever? The records we have still to hand have much to say about Lot!

HIDDEN TREASURE: *HOPE*

Some seemingly inviting waters will never slake the soul's thirst.

A WORD FROM THE WORD

תקוה
tiqvah – "expectation"

Travellers need an able, stable, endurance "vehicle" in sandy soil. The camel I encountered, on the coast of South Australia, appeared to me to be either bleating its displeasure at "water, water everywhere, but not a drop to drink", or smirking at the humour of the occasion. Obviously, the camel had been on a journey in the company of its now absent keeper. It was most unusual to find any camels so far south for, normally, a host of feral camels—an introduced species—roamed the vast wilderness of Central Australia. But this camel "made my day"!

A VIEWPOINT TO PONDER
How could a thirsty human soul find hope?

The body receives its fluid requirement with water. The mind is kept active by the intake of ideas, concepts to increase knowledge and is invigorated. The soul finds refreshment by acquiring Truth, which leads to Faith, the progenitor of Hope!

PILGRIM'S JOURNAL: Genesis 12:1–9

This pilgrim does not know if camels were employed by Abram and the team journeying with him at the time. Donkeys, maybe? Or, the travellers set out on their epic journey on foot? Whatever, the camel does allow us to settle into the journey with a strong sense of affinity with the obvious challenges to be endured on this journey. One thing we do know: Abram and Sarai were not alone on their epic pilgrimage.

The extant records in Genesis provide, in surprising detail, the personnel involved: Abram and Sarai, their nephew, Lot, of course. And, the text informs us, the group was enlarged by personnel that had been "accumulated" in Haran—people with ample means: we are informed that Abram had accumulated many possessions and this would be good reason for a number of slaves, servants, or associates to be accompanying the master, now the owner of much wealth.

Often, such personnel were employed on a voluntary basis. In the circumstances now under observation, it would seem most probable that the travellers included people who were desirous of making the journey in the company of Abram and Sarai so that they also might share in possible wealth. But Abram's true riches were not possessions packed away in the saddle bags. Above and beyond all wealth would be carried the gem of **hope**! The pilgrims would never have left the safe environs of Haran without the hope engendered by the promise of *YHVH* to this awe-inspiring faithful patriarch. There were many possessions in the saddle bags, but there was hope in the heart.

How is hope included as a spiritual possession? There is a vast difference between the verb and the noun! The verb is the action word that would have us declare (with a measure of uncertainty), "I hope that I will be able to complete the course." The noun, however, is built of stronger stuff! One can be heard to declare, with the certainty born of experience, "my hope is built on the strong foundation of the faith I have in the LORD. He has promised to guard and to guide me and I mean to follow on. He keeps His word." Do you hear Abram here? I do!

THE REFLECTIVE GLANCE

IT IS GOOD TO PAUSE A MOMENT
AS THE FAITH OF ABRAM IS ENCOUNTERED,
FOR IT IS THE VERY FOUNDATION OF
THE HOPE HE HELD IN THE LORD.

* FAITH'S VISION

*Faith brings the ample evidence
Of boundless things not seen or heard
For, with the eyes and ears of faith,
Our inner sense of Truth is stirred.*

*Faith brings ability to trust
Though clouds obscure the path ahead;
Its vision sees, beyond the night,
That light will dawn and doubt be dead.*

*Faith brings assurances that all
The promises of God are real,
The promise known: the promise claimed;
Such gifting will God's grace reveal.*

*Faith brings the access into grace
Wherein we stand and we rejoice
In hope of all God's glory here;
His love outpoured is matchless grace!*

*Faith brings the knowledge that all things
Will work together for the good,
The ultimate great victory,
Of all whose trust is in the LORD!*

This poem—set in L.M.—may be sung as a hymn:
e.g. *Old Hundreth.* Related Scripture: Romans 5:1–5, 8:28.

THE FORWARD GLANCE

MUCH IS SAID IN COMMENDATION
REGARDING THE FAITH OF ABRAM AND HE
IS WORTHY OF EVERY WORD! HOWEVER, LITTLE
IS SAID OF THE FAITHFULNESS OF SARAI. THIS
PILGRIMAGE LIFTS THAT GEM TO OUR GAZE
AND IT REMINDS THE PILGRIM OF:

* GOD'S FAITHFULNESS

Wonderful God's faithfulness!
Ever present with His care;
When the way is dark ahead,
I have found Him to be there.

Precious is God's faithfulness
And He's gifted me with faith
Every challenge to engage
As I walk life's daily path.

Steadfast is God's faithfulness!
Though I might His will defy,
Still His faithfulness remains:
God will not Himself deny.

Trusting in God's faithfulness
There is hope for what's to be;
Standing on His promises,
Faith in action strengthens me.

God has called to faithfulness,
All the days of pilgrimage.
Echo of His faith in me,
Faith is found to serve this age.

God has called me to this hope
All the days of pilgrimage.
He has found in me a faith
That will stand in this our age.

Another hymn for the journey: 7.7.7.7. e.g. *Nottingham*

HIDDEN TREASURE: *COMPANIONS*

The tallest tree will always be a signpost for the pilgrim.

A WORD FROM THE WORD

נפש
nephesh – "persons"

At the southern end of my family home in Crabtree, Tasmania, was a giant of a tree. It was truly magnificent, of sublime shape, and as good a signpost as this little daughter of the Turfrey Clan ever needed to know: as soon as we were over the brow of the hill, we were almost home. The tree was known as "The Ivy Tree"! It took some years to realise that our tree was no tree at all! The truth of the matter finally dawned on me. Ivy would never grow into a tree, but it does know how to cling to that which has stability. The tree that challenged me to take some paint to canvas was a tree that stood sentinel to its companions in a fertile valley in the red desert lands of Central Australia!

A VIEWPOINT TO PONDER
How can ivy become a signpost to home?

If the inner stabiliser is strong enough, reaches high enough, is welcoming enough, and provides its companion a place to dwell it will. Inner strength provides ivy with a happy abiding place.

There are those—including some notable wise men—who will follow a guiding star. Many will rely on the trusted signposts (always a reliable aid to grant the guidance required along the chosen route). Pilgrims are more aware—many from personal experience—of the sure "inner compass" that leads unerringly to the goal to which they are called. The synonym most appropriate—and most related—is "vocation". It is a calling that has motivated Abram and his **companions** to scan the horizons again, marking a new phase in the epic journey.

In facing the unknown yet again, it had surely dawned upon the company that the way ahead would be fraught with challenges not yet encountered on their previous trek. All were, however, experiencing the mighty reinforcement of the intention that hope, built on faith, adds strength to the human soul.

The companions (always a gem for the depth of fellowship that it gifts), continued to travel for a time through the Fertile Crescent. Then, as they stepped into "alien" territory, known to be the Land of Canaan, one would have thought that the journey had reached a satisfying conclusion. But Abram did not erect his tents! The company continued southward—perhaps, at times, just a day's march from The Great Middle Sea.

Genesis 12:6 informs us that Abram (and his entourage) *travelled on south until they reached the site of the great tree of Moreh* (perhaps later becoming known as Shechem). A much later insert in the record mentions an event at this site when Abram's grandson (Jacob), buried some foreign gods "under the tree at Shechem"! Obviously, this was a very well-known tree and it is widely thought to be "the great tree of Moreh".

It appears that the great tree at Moreh was treated as a signpost to mark the location of gods worshipped by the Canaanites. It was here that *YHVH* was now worshipped in Canaan! The LORD made it a special place for He appeared to Abram at worship, to reaffirm His great promise (12:7). This strategic event leads on to a site that would become known as Bethel!!!

HIDDEN TREASURE: *RESOURCES*

A table, even if a mountain, offers sparse fare in the desert.

A WORD FROM THE WORD

כּוּל
kul – "provision"

The table is bare, but not quite. There is food, nourishing food to be found—if one knows where to look. High on the desert fare is the cactus! Once past the spikes, the fluid is nutritious. The prickly pear should be mentioned, the agave, dates, olives, aloes, gourds, berries, yucca and the nourishment gained from the sap dripping from the ash tree (though these trees could be scarce). The hot sun solidifies the syrup into a white sponge-like substance that is very sweet, therefore high in short-term energy intake. Meat is sparse but Abram and his companions would have herded large flocks of sheep and goats. Also, feral animals would have roamed the waste-land.

A VIEWPOINT TO PONDER
What would attract anyone to desert country?

There are a number of reasons: spectacular viewing, wide, open spaces, colourful scenery, and: to get to the other side!

PILGRIM'S JOURNAL: Genesis 12:6–20

What attracted Abram and his entourage to travel south into the Negev? Good question! Possibly, one reason was that they didn't know what the country ahead offered them. It is on record, however, that there was a famine! Why, oh why, did not the men observe that the grass is not greener in a desert?

The safer option, perhaps, would have been to "about turn", and head once more into the Fertile Crescent until the famine was past. Indeed, Abram possessed wonderful **resources**—those given into his hand and heart by *YHVH*:

YHVH appeared—appeared—*to Abram at the great tree of Moreh at Shechem and added to His prior promise: 'I will give this land to your children!'* (v. 7).

It should be remembered that Sarai had no children! This land was to be gifted—to at the time—non-existent children. Abram's faith surely should have been lifted to a higher plane! Yes, Abram was aware of the wonderful resources that were his through trusting God. But he failed to be resourceful in his decision-making at crucial times: First, he decided to take the company into the southern Negev desert; secondly—being dissatisfied with what he found—the intrepid traveller turned due west and landed in Egypt! Help!!!

The instruction he gave to Sarai is appalling, as Genesis 12:10–20 explains so vividly. Surely, it is only because of the continuing care of *YHVH* that brought him, his beloved, and the entire troupe out of the clutches of Pharoah. Yes, Abram already possessed the resource—the gem—that would have seen a better result had he remained in the Promised Land. But Abram failed to act with resourcefulness. He would need to do better in the future by taking *YHVH* at His word!

As we enter chapter 13, it will be discovered that Abram possessed the superb resource of kindness as he ceded his right to the better country. Lot was given the option of choosing which option to take. His selfishness led him to disaster! Lot had feasted his eyes on the "best". His greed led him to Sodom.

HIDDEN TREASURE: *WORSHIP*

A pasture where sheep may graze brings satisfaction to the shepherd.

A WORD FROM THE WORD

שׁחה

shachah – "worship"

Stanley bought a prize ram. Magnificent creature, Stanley's ram "knocked" at our front door one day and it was all I could do to dissuade it from demanding morning tea in our front room! Stanley did not come easily to the skills of a shepherd. He tried, most inefficiently to *drive* his flock to new pastures but the sheep were most recalcitrant. That shepherd was slow to learn the basic principle that sheep will *follow* a good shepherd.

A VIEWPOINT TO PONDER
Is it not possible to be a good drover?

Well, a shepherd who knows the value of a well-trained sheep dog—for example, the Border Collie—will find that the sheep soon discover who is in charge and so behave immaculately.

Abram was soon to discover that his kind action toward Lot had in fact enabled him to find green pastures again! Abram and his companions came to a most pleasant setting in Canaan where the LORD appeared to him once again:

Abram, lift your eyes: look to the north, to the south, to the east and to the west. This is the land I am giving to you! Your descendants will be as numerous as sand by the sea-shore. Go, walk through the land, it will be yours! (Ch. 13:14–17).

Abram then moved his tents to settle by the great trees "signposting" Mamre, a magnificent area where his entourage could settle in Hebron. Abram had come "Home"! His response to the revelation of the LORD was to build an altar. Abram was purposing to **worship** *YHVH*. He was following the highest calling of his life: Abram had discovered the gem of communion!

People who continue to utilise the vital link of prayer are prone to live by, and act by, the directions that emerge in the mind, the soul, of those faithful to *YHVH*. Here is *worth*-ship!

Chapter 14 leads into disquieting news concerning Lot which prompted Abram to step into the fray to free his nephew. It is here that Abram is first referred to as being a Hebrew. He thus becomes the Father of this people. It was following this struggle that the king of Salem (that is, Jerusalem!), goes out to greet Abram, taking with him food and wine. The honoured name of this king was Melchizedek—meaning "king of righteousness". His greeting is superb:

May you be blessed by the Most High God, the Creator of heaven and Earth. And praise be to God Most High who has delivered your enemies into your hand. (Ch. 14:19–20).

There are many conjectures as to who this king really was. We focus on his friendly hospitality. Abram responded in a most significant way as he offers a tenth of all his spoils of battle! Here we are confronted with a special solemnity of thanksgiving: the tithe! The raised hand signified the promise.

HIDDEN TREASURE: *COMMITMENT*

Outcomes of promises are shrouded in mystery, needing clear vision

A WORD FROM THE WORD

דָּבַר

dabar – "speak"

It was only a minor misdemeanour. Surely not sufficient to raise the ire of my mother. Yet here I was, absconding from home! The day was benign. I made the most of my new-found freedom touring the island to the south of our property. This was my new abode. Food? There was the peach tree, the plum tree and, apples close by. But evening closed in. Where were my blankets? My bed? I returned home. In facing up to my mother, I announced, 'Mother, I'm sorry. I won't do that again.' Years later when holidaying with my parents, my mother reminded me of the occasion and my promise. 'You didn't behave like that again. You kept your word. You were different from that day on.'

A VIEWPOINT TO PONDER
How does one turn a promise into an action?

It takes resolve, will-power, and faithfulness. Translate words into deeds so that what you promise, you will fulfil: you will DO!

It is possible that you are asking why the Hidden Treasure—**commitment**—and the selected word from the original language are so different. The matter is resolved by the realisation that, in the time of Abram, to give one's word by way of a promise was tantamount to the action done! The ancient "Picture Parables" certainly provide hints of this: ד is the doorway, "open" to the quest; ב is to be "in the home", ready to fulfil the deed; ר is the head: to have a mind to activate the promise, in the soul the resolve to be as good as one's word!

In observing the chapters under review with the purpose of digging below the superficial soil, readers will be amazed at the number of times that *YHVH* reiterates His promise that the land of Canaan would be gifted to Abram's family! What family? Where is the family of Abram?

Doubts arose! Sarai took matters into her hands and caused the terrible debacle with Hagar because she really wanted her Abram to be a father. Sarai forgot that the LORD was working through that process! The resultant son, Ishmael and his descendants, have been a "thorn-in-the-flesh" since his birth! It is certainly wonderful to find the forgiveness of God in all these unfortunate events—as Genesis 16 explains so well.

As we enter chapter 17, the promises of God to Abram reach a new height! This promise is balanced by a request. The wonder of this meeting is all but lost to the "tourist" traveller. Dig below the surface of the soil. See what the original language makes of: *I am El Shaddai—God, the Almighty One—walk before Me and be blameless:* הלך = *Walk*   לפני = *before My Face*   והיה = *and be*   תמים = *perfect, blameless, whole.*

Quality of life is now asked of Abram! English translations have toned down the request of God—*El Shaddai, God Almighty* (the new name that God disclosed). God is here asking Abram to now walk *before His Face and to live a perfect life!* How? Live to fulfil God's will: love Him, serve Him, and enjoy Him forever!

HIDDEN TREASURE: *INTERCESSION*

Trees and people that stand tall are those who reach out to all.

A WORD FROM THE WORD

ארשת

aresheth – "request"

In a valley surrounded by forests, it is not surprising that trees warmed my heart! And, of course, our log fires warmed our homes on a snowy, winter's night! There was the "ivy tree" that stood as the signpost to our farm; there was the crab-apple tree that named our little valley, and there was the magnificent eucalypt that stood taller than all else and caught the attention of everyone, proclaiming: "come, you are not far from home."

A VIEWPOINT TO PONDER
How can a tree on the brow of a hill stand so tall?

Facing west, the tree must withstand the worst of winter's wind-blown storms. Withstanding storms gives the tree its strength.

Who were those men? First, let me set the scene. Abram has received an update on his name: he is now to be known as Abraham—*father of multitudes. A*nd Sarai is to be known as Sarah—*princess.* Abraham is seated under the beloved trees at Mamre, and Sarah is busy in the tent with homely matters.

Three men arrive. They are greeted most hospitably and Abraham requests his wife to prepare a repast for the visitors. The content of the conversation (provided in intricate detail in Genesis 18), causes Sarah to laugh scornfully for the coming of a child has been announced! At the same time, Abraham is beginning to wonder if the visitors are ordinary men.

As the visitors take their leave following the luncheon, Abraham elects to walk with them in order to show respect. One of the visitors is not unknown to Abraham! He recognises the voice for they have met frequently—when Abraham has been engaged in prayer! Here is yet another occasion when the pilgrim has come face to Face, spiritually speaking, with the LORD!

It is opportune to indicate here that there are, in the Old Testament, significant occasions when the pre-existent Jesus is met (see John 1:1–14). *He was **in the beginning** with God and, He was* (and IS) *God…* John's great Prologue sets the matter straight. Abraham was experiencing a theophany! God was actually present at that luncheon. No wonder Abraham walked with the Trio. The other men are thought to be angels).

When Abraham is made aware of the intention to wipe the sins of Sodom and Gomorrah from the face of the Earth, he engages in what remains one of the greatest prayers of **intercession** ever recorded. Abraham pleads, continues to plead. The LORD's willingness to respond favourably is wonderful—a gem indeed. But for their sins, the cities were lost. Refusal to comply with decency demanded retribution. Though every effort was made by Heaven's men, Lot lost his wife to salt, a "monument" which remained as a beacon to failure.

A Gem – Abraham

THE PILGRIM

First, let me introduce
myself again. You'll know
me as Abram. Now Abraham!
You see, I'm going to be a "dad",
I'll be the abba Abraham, for
I am to father sons at last!
and, many more, so far from kith
and kin, my sons—and daughters, too,
of course, will be as numberless
as shifting sand upon the shore
of seas beyond the far horizons
of this precious promised land.
(My Sarah laughed).

He greeted me one day,
the *El Shaddai—God, the
Almighty One*—had asked
of me to walk within the Light
of His own Face! He asked of me
a perfect life of true integrity…
He came to me when I was all
of ninety-nine! He said that He
would make with me a pact—
a Covenant. It would take two
to make these promises: He'd keep
His own and asked that I hold faith.
(My Sarah laughed).

I sit within my tent to muse
beneath the favoured terebinth—
the tree that sentinels the plains
from far beyond. I call this home.
So, let me see, the men were three.
My hospitality received so well,

THE PILGRIM

they sat at ease with me,
they questioned me, they surely
challenged me on many things;
they spoke of our first son.
(My Sarah laughed).

The One of three—that sat
to chat with me that day—
his Light-filled eyes reminded me...
My LORD! I knew that gaze
within my heart; that Face of Light
is known to me today! It warmed
my heart to see Him now. His eyes
held mine. I thought again
of promises and Covenant.
He spoke my new-known name!
(My Sarah laughed).

A multitude, like as the sands,
the numberless grained sands,
much more than these?
And I? the doubt was strong,
yet I recalled the promises
once given by the El Shaddai.
So, as the drifting sands,
the countless stars, my sons
of sons to be? A child
for Sarah and for me?
The gifts of God are limitless:
I know it now for I'll hold faith.
(My Sarah laughed).

One glorious, child-birth day,
my Sarah will rejoice. You see,
her laugh will be transformed by JOY!

HIDDEN TREASURE: *FULFILMENT*

An insignificant juxtaposition may hide a monumental reality.

A WORD FROM THE WORD

מלא
mala: "fulfill"

"When you go to Oxford, be sure to visit the Monument to the Martyrs in the Broad." I knew to whom my principal referred. At the time I was studying in London. As the course drew to a close, I arranged, with some student friends, to journey north. Actually, my goal was to move on to Eynsham, from whence my great-grandfather was taken as a convict to the notorious prison at Port Arthur, Tasmania. But where was the monument? No help was forthcoming from two professors at the university. Then another came forward: "It depends on what you're looking for." And he told me. Just outside the gate, in the middle of the famous "Broad", was the cross which marks the very place where Hugh Ridley and Nicolas Latimer were burned at the stake because they would not relinquish their faith in Christ.

A VIEWPOINT TO PONDER
Why surrender one's life for an inner conviction of faith?

The decision has eternal consequences—from death to LIFE!

It has happened! Hallelujah! A son has been born to Abraham and Sarah. The gift was the **fulfilment** of God's promise to her and to the father, both of whom were overcome by the event. They were discovering much about the way that God always keeps His promises. A difficult name to pronounce in the original, the little boy is best known as Isaac. Sarah's comment that his coming caused laughter could not have referred to her smirk when overhearing the heavenly visitors. Sarah knew joy!

Abraham and Sarah's pilgrimage was packed full of dramatic incidents. Hagar and Ishmael have been dismissed but the record in Genesis 20:8–21 tells of how the LORD did not abandon them! Abraham and Sarah had now moved from Mamre and found themselves embroiled once more in an event that proved to be so very similar to the Egyptian fiasco.

Readers will be interested to note that the name Abimelech means *father of the king*, and Beersheba (a place name that has stood the test of time being one of the oldest remaining Canaanite locations today), means *well of the promise.*

When digging below the many details on record, one must not overlook the major test to Abraham's faith. It is a difficult story and one for which serious students must work hard to come to terms with its ramifications. How could it be that *YHVH* would ask such an outlandish request of Abraham? Has the recorder got the facts straight? But yes! Abraham lived in an age when such a sacrifice was part of the religious culture of surrounding nations who had no belief in the One True God! It would seem that the challenge to Abraham was to test if he was prepared to go to that ultimate extreme of delivering up the son he loved (and Sarah, don't forget Sarah's grief)! See Chapter 22.

The facts are astounding! Where did Abraham take his son for sacrifice? To Mount Moriah—the site of what would become Jerusalem—where another beloved "Son" one day would give His life as the "Lamb caught in a thicket", nailed to a cross! Yes, God would provide the Lamb—slain for the world on Calvary!

HIDDEN TREASURE: *LIFE*

A late-comer to life, a tenacious plant will thrive by reaching for light.

A WORD FROM THE WORD

חיה
chayah – "to be alive"

On assignment in Russia, I suddenly became quite ill. Due for my annual vacation, I had arranged a London holiday with friends. This occasioned a medical examination where a rare life-threatening tumour was discovered. Specialist opinion had it that I must return immediately to Australia as recovery from surgery would be an extended process. Life in Moscow was no longer viable. It was acknowledged that, should the cabin pressure lower during the flight, I probably would not make it to Melbourne. A routine check-up had sent shock-waves through my vacation and, more-so, my vocation. But I live on!

A VIEWPOINT TO PONDER
How do we conquer the shock of life-threatening news?

Prayer before fronting up to the situation strengthens faith. Trust the surgeon's abilities, trust your own capacities, know that it is the body's ability to heal itself. And, have faith in God!

Isaac is one of the unsung heroes of the Old Testament! The superficial scan of his life gives us just the bare outline. But a little digging, here and there, will disclose some magnificent gems! Take **life** itself. Life for Isaac was not easy!

Isaac's parents—Abraham and Sarah—were aged before his birth according to the ancient means of assessing age and years. In his infancy and youth, Isaac would have been rather a lonely lad. And, there was that moment when he feared for his very life at the hand of his father! Faith, and love, saw the crisis through to its wonderful conclusion. Sarah had died some years before Abraham. Therefore, Isaac lived much of his earlier life without his mother's tender, loving care.

According to custom, it was the responsibility of the father to arrange the marriage of his son. Isaac was going to marry no alien! His bride would come from a family connection. A servant was called and the instructions given must surely have caused the man to quail!

It is so very heart-warming to find that the servant carried in his heart an active faith in God! The plan of the man was not birthed in the mind of his employer. Through prayer, the servant conceived an approach that would make the choice an affective one. And, the plan could not have worked out better. Rebekah's kindness at the first meeting, her courage when it came to decision-making time makes her also an outstanding heroin of the Old Testament. The meeting, the marriage, and the lives of Isaac and Rebekah, were superb—that is, until old age.

Isaac's reaction to adverse conditions is remarkable. When neighbours—be they friend or foe—would refuse access to the vital resource of life—a well—one is staggered at this early instance of man's inhumanity to man. What did Isaac do? He moved to new ground, had dug a new well. "Neighbours" blocked access. Isaac moved on. His wells were seized once more. On the edge of life itself, Isaac stood tall! Then, no more confrontations. Enemies became friends—at Beersheba!

HIDDEN TREASURE: *BEERSHEBA*

What a glory is discovered when water finds its place in the desert.

A WORD FROM THE WORD

בְּאֵר שֶׁבַע

beer-sheba – "well of the promise"

It was yet early morning and my friend and I had already traversed some distance along the sandy trail as we absorbed the grandeur or this arid land. And there it was—an oasis to greet us. Central Australia may be considered desert country, but its "red heart" is alive. We were overcome by a spectacular arbour in the desert that shouts its colour in a crescendo that would evoke the soul's response to God who lends its life to all who ensure that no flood, or fire, or famine may destroy it now.

A POINT TO PONDER
How may such magnificent beauty be found in a desert?

The indigenous people of Australia have cared for, nurtured this country for countless years. They know their land and care for it. They know its worth for it has sustained them through time. And, so should the "late-comers" to the land also care for it.

Beersheba is first mentioned in Genesis when Abraham made a covenant with Abimelech, a Philistine king. He had bargained with the king and came to an amicable arrangement, making their covenant at a well of water! The reason for the negotiations was because of that well—one of the most famous of all wells, not only for its significance for Abraham and the Philistines. The **Well of the Promise** still holds significance for it has ensured, throughout the on-going centuries, the viability of **Beersheba** in this, the 21st Century! Beersheba is one of the most ancient settlements still viable today! The key word is "water"!

My personal joy in Beersheba stems from the fact that the museum was closed that day. I looked through the iron frame barring the doorway to observe an ancient Canaanite altar. I was observed. A conversation took place. I mentioned the altar's antiquity and so was introduced to the archaeologist who had discovered the altar acclaimed to be the most ancient yet uncovered from the earth, dating back to the 8th Century BC.

Of greater import is the Battle of Beersheba which took place on 31 October, 1917, with the historic charge of the Australian Light Horse Brigade, taking the enemy by surprise and securing the Sinai Peninsula. In doing so, they ensured the necessary shipping corridors along the Suez Canal for all the Allied Forces in the entire region. This magnificent victory helped to turn the tide of WW1. The Battle for Beersheba had secured the region's only reliable water supply, giving over 60,000 troops access to the famous water, and providing me with good reason to include this account of the famous Battle of Beersheba.

The well, the "Beersheba", is first mentioned when Abraham bargained with Abimelech, making their Covenant of Peace at that well of water! And Isaac repeated such a bargain with probably the same king (though the name could be hereditary).

Beersheba stands on the last fertile land before the Negev Desert. This is truly an oasis of historic importance and no doubt has brought countless joy to many through the ages!

THE REFLECTIVE GLANCE

THE ACCOUNT OF ABRAHAM'S WILLINGNESS
TO SACRIFICE HIS OWN SON AT MOUNT MORIAH
TO PROVE HIS FAITH IN *YHVH* HAS REVEALED GOD'S
WILLINGNESS TO SACRIFICE HIS SON. ISAIAH'S
PROPHECY DESCRIBES CALVARY'S DAY:

* THE SUFFERING SERVANT
Isaiah 53   Tune: e.g. *Chalvey*   D.S.M.

Who has believed our word,
To whom is God made known?
Grown like a root from driest ground,
No majesty is shown.
Despised, rejected, sad,
We all had passed Him by,
But He has borne our many griefs,
Was smitten, left to die.

The Lord was pierced for us,
And crushed for what we've done!
He carried sin to bring us peace,
Through death, He did atone.
All we like sheep have strayed,
We turned from Him away!
The Lord has laid upon His soul
All our iniquity.

He silent came to death,
Like unto lambs, was slain:
His tomb aligned with wickedness
Though He had done no sin.
Yet after death comes life,
His soul is satisfied!
Because through death
He bore our sins,
Our soul is satisfied.

THE FORWARD GLANCE

WHILE ISAIAH'S GREAT "PSALM"
LIES IN THE FIELD OF PROPHECY, IT IS IN THE
NEW TESTAMENT THAT THE "PICTURE
PARABLE" IN GENESIS IS FULFILLED.

* THE SHADOW OF DEATH
John 19:17–37   Tune: e.g. *Who is He?*   7.7.7.7.7.7.

Darkness shadowed all the Earth
When our Lord was crucified,
Day became the darkest night,
Nature sorrowed in the gloom.
Sun and moon retired to grieve,
Veiled from the Eternal Light.

Death had entered in this scene,
Strident in its rampant might;
Purity was slaughtered here.
Righteousness was overthrown
By satanic powers unleashed;
Gone from us our Saviour dear.

He was taken to the cross,
Raised upon its awful frame;
Who selected such a death
For a man so innocent?
Who willed Jesus Christ to die?
Who? The Lord of Heaven and Earth!

God sent not His only Son
To the world, there to condemn
Earth in every passing phase,
His great Gift would save the world;
Calvary was meant for me,
But in grace, Christ took my place.

When He cried, 'Abba, it's done!'
Jesus knew accomplishment;
Satan would not claim this day;
Not the victor, death was done!
Never would it conqueror be,
Never dim God's radiant day!

127

HIDDEN TREASURE: *HOUSE OF GOD*

The skies will display the glory of God to those who take note of it.

A WORD FROM THE WORD

ביתאל
bethel – "House of God"

My dad was an "Isaac" of a man. And mother stood at his side as the ideal Rebekah! There was little to count by way of possessions. But they did possess a house, a house that became home to the parents and their children. The eight children were individuals. One brother possessed a fiery temper, another had an engaging grin, used frequently. Also, my sisters and I were dramatically different in our likes and dislikes but we lived together amicably. Our family loved our home! And our lives were the better for the discipline of parents who knew that the "house of God" was of benefit for who we were and would become. A humble, weather-board hall was the birth place of our faith. I will be forever thankful for this 'home'!

A VIEWPOINT TO PONDER
What makes a house into a home?

A home is not constructed with tent pegs or cement. A home has *soul*, the soul of a family in touch with each other and God.

With the advent of Jacob and Esau—actually, that should be Esau and Jacob as the text of 25:19–34 plainly shows—into the home tent of Isaac and Rebekah, a new phase has opened up in history's page relating to the story of the Hebrew nation. The lives of these personalities are of great importance. They remain as major participants in the accounting of how God has repeatedly acted to rectify humanity's inability to live according to the moral, ethical and spiritual code set out for them from Eden's "day", through all their migrations, and settling down.

As for Esau and Jacob, it is indeed a sorry tale though neither lad, presumably, would have been sorry for their many misdemeanours and, more to the point, their sins. Jacob could not rectify the order in which he departed his mother's womb but he could have done better to rectify his attitude toward his brother and, with his own young life, than to earn the title "deceiver". Look where it landed him.

Finally, Jacob's subterfuge gained the better of him for he went a step too far! Of greater loss than the shelter of the tents housing the family, Jacob—suddenly—was deprived of the home life that surrounded and supported the recalcitrant youth. He must say a sad farewell to his parents: Isaac, now blind with age and in continuing need of his sons, and Rebekah who must reap the bitter harvest of her obvious preference of the younger lad. Jacob was now an outcast from home.

Jacob beds down on an uncompromising landscape with nought but a stone to rest his head when, suddenly, the skies above shone with the Light of Heaven! The dreamer was shaken into an awareness beyond that of earthly realities. An astounding stairway gave access for Heaven's angels to descend and ascend, making way for the appearance of the LORD! When God makes Himself known, He speaks His will, makes known His promises. Jacob heard but did he listen? He recognised the LORD: he realised this place was holy: '*This is "Bethel"* "**House of God**!" But Jacob did not change his ways.

Basking in one's enterprises will fail to develop a worthy aim.

A WORD FROM THE WORD

חבק

chabaq – "a welcoming embrace"

My sister Naomi's frog is the epitome of 'look at me, how good am I?!' This frog lounged by the fountain, basking in the sun, displaying his self-satisfaction for all to see. There was not much else the frog could do, being of the porcelain variety! He was also of the "Jacob" variety. Which brings one to the leopard: can a leopard change its spots? The thing is, a leopard can change the spots where it chooses to linger but a leopard is a leopard, wherever he chooses to move and rest awhile.

A VIEWPOINT TO PONDER
Is not a choice made on the basis of what I want or need?

Correct! Most choices, that is. The shopping bag is filled with groceries desired, required, to fill the plate. However, a person in touch with spiritual verities, will be aware of what others need.

Jacob had been welcomed at the home of his forebears with open arms. Literally! He received a welcoming **embrace** from his relative! And here we find the submerged gem, lying just beneath the surface of the soil! Here is opportunity for life to begin again with a better set of values than those displayed at home in Beersheba—and, with the impetus offered at Bethel.

Upon arrival, Jacob is surprised to see a well—the centre of attention of the flocks restive in the field—blocked by a large stone. The shepherds come then to check on the visitor. Then, the shepherdess. Jacob is smitten with love at first sight! Here was Rachel who was to become the love of his life. Introductions were made and Jacob was assured that he had "come home"! Jacob did the honourable thing!!! He rolled the stone away. And then, he kissed Rachel! She was "family".

Jacob was invited to meet with Laban, his mother's brother (and father of Rachel). Laban's welcome is effusive and warm. There was much rejoicing in the family tents. Here was Jacob's opportunity to change his ways. He was eager to assist the family enterprise in any way he could. Here was his extended family. Also, Rachel! And, Laban appreciated the lad. "Should you be working for me without payment? Tell me, what should I pay you?" Jacob, wily Jacob, saw his chance: a salary with a bonus! "May I marry your daughter, Rachel, if I work for you for seven years?"

There was a problem looming on Jacob's joy—the elder sister with "delicate" eye-sight. By right, the elder daughter should marry first. And such was the outcome of the marriage: Jacob woke in the marriage bed to find Leah!!!

"What have you done? I've served you well and this is how you pay me?" A compromise was made. Within a short space of time, Jacob found himself with two wives. He also found ways and means to deceive the deceiver! Jacob had remained true to type. In the end, his subterfuge necessitated a hurried exit, with wives and his amassed wealth. Jacob was going "home"!

HIDDEN TREASURE: *REPENTANCE*

After the darkest night a new dawn will arrive with its sunlight.

A WORD FROM THE WORD

נחם

nacham – "repentance, regret wrongs"

Safely aloft on the last sector of my flight home from Russia, it was a joy to observe the dawn rising above the dense clouds that had served to deepen the darkness of the night. Here was hope, shining through my window. A new dawn was breaking. The night had held the "clouds" of devastating news. What would tomorrow hold? Then, came the dawn! The rising sun spoke its golden truth to me, here was a new dawn. Whatever the future held, its was also holding my faith in the LORD.

A VIEWPOINT TO PONDER
What is it about light that allows for a change of mind?

The matter under discussion does not relate to what is seen with the eyes. Sunlight helps us, however, to see where we are. Enlightenment enables us to see who we are and what we are!

As Jacob and his entourage neared the home he had known and loved all those years ago, his anticipation increased. But he also thought of Esau's precedence in the family affections—while he was Rebekah's pride and joy, Esau was favoured by his father, Isaac. Then the news was delivered that Esau was approaching in the company of four hundred men. Jacob knew the old fear and the antagonisms of the past surfacing once more. It was time to act "judicially" if he was to save himself!

Four hundred men? It was time for some Jacob jabs! Plans were hastily set in place. Jacob's entourage would meet up with Esau but he would abscond into the hills to think of further ploys. His people and the flocks were divided into two groups (perhaps one would be saved). He then prepared a substantial gift to appease his brother. Jacob neared the Jabbok stream with his wives and eleven sons. He sent all across, then his possessions. But he, the wily Jacob, stayed behind in the hope, perhaps, that Esau would be placated.

However, something else happened that very night. Something new! Jacob went aside to pray, earnestly pray! Here was the sign of the "new dawn", the gem in the saga! *O God of my fathers, of my father Isaac, You who promised even me, 'go back to your family and I will make you prosper,' LORD, I am unworthy of Your kindness and faithfulness to me…*

A "New Dawn" was about to break. But first, the struggle with that Unknown Entity. Left alone, Jacob was accosted by a Man with whom he wrestled through the night. Near morning, Jacob's opponent asked to be released for He knew that Jacob was not about to give up the "fight"! *'Let me go, for day is now upon us!'* And Jacob replied: *I won't let go unless You bless me!* Jacob had recognised his opponent And, he named the site, *PENIEL*: the *Face of God!* This said everything! And, Jacob became *ISRAEL*! People's lives can change, when they **repent** of their wrongs and are prepared to have the LORD put them right—Jacob, *deceiver,* can become Israel: *prevailing with God.*

A Gem – Jacob-Israel

THE TRANSFORMED

I've been redeemed!
From all my past: redeemed!
The old man, yes, the "Jacob"
that was me. You see, I've been
re-claimed! I had no pride
in what was me but shackles held
me fast in what was me.
Just once, or twice, perhaps,
I'd tried to change. But how
can one man change himself?!

I've been forgiven!
My "Jacob" ways had wounded
many people through the years—
my wives and sons as well, I fear.
Released at last, at no great cost—
except my pride—I'm free!
You'll see no more the "Jacob" way
within; though none might tell
but for this smile, this warmth
in me. I feel the Light of God
upon my weather-beaten face!

I've been renewed!
The struggle of the night was long!
I wrestled with this One who came,
on eve, to challenge me though what
the looming challenge was, I scarce
can tell. He met His match, He did!
Though, in the victory there, I felt
as in the Home of God, the Man
more agile and of awesome strength—
much more than I who fought
Him through that blackest night!

THE TRANSFORMED

I've been transformed!
I chose to struggle on until
He blessed me whole!
This ground is now known
as the *"Peniel"* for, yes,
I've seen the *"Face of God"*
and yet I live to tell of it!
I've looked with awe into
those searching eyes and knew
He'd righted all the wrongs,
my grievous wrongs. I'm whole!

I've been reborn!
I'm now *'Israel'*, for I am "new"!
I am *"prevailing with my God"*.
Could any slip again into
his mother's womb? To be
reborn, receive another chance
to live again without the pains
of what is past of sins and all
those misdemeanours, sins,
for selfish gain? This is indeed
a miracle upon my soul!

I've been received!
received into "the family
of God". I know, within
the heart of me, a birth again,
a life that's new, through this
encounter with the LORD!
Yet, who could tell, but for
my limp—the "wonder wound"
of Elohim, upon my hip? I limp!
I know it now: He won the fight!
He changed my life around:
I'll be a blessing to my family now!

HIDDEN TREASURE: *REBUKE*

Those who climb mountains should choose appropriate footwear.

A WORD FROM THE WORD

גְּעָר

gaar – "rebuke"

In searching for an adequate excuse, let it be said I did not start the day with any thought of sitting on a mountain-top, facing a sheer drop of mountainous proportions. And no, I did not undertake to climb the mountain anyway. It was done the easy way—merely alighting from our hire car when feasting our eyes upon Yosemite National Park, USA, from the "high" way! That I should be granted such a view as this is astounding. We had travelled the valley in comfort and now, to complete the journey by observing Half Dome Rock and its adjacent famous water-fall, was a highlight of the journey. Casual shoes were hardly appropriate even to perch upon a mountain-top! And, for life's journey: certainly, be shod with Peace! (See Ephesians 6:15).

A VIEWPOINT TO PONDER
Why is it so vital to wear a pair of "Peace Shoes"?

The moral is, with families and with nations, we should be ready to become peacemakers. "A soft answer turns away wrath!"

Jacob and Leah's lads were unpleasant boys and, as they grew, they became most unpleasant men! It must be accepted that, when young and most impressionable, they had failed to find in their dad, an example worth their stepping into his sandalled footprints. More than a little too late, these lads earned the ire of their father for their deeds found no excuse and the **rebuke** they received should have made for better relationships. Was it too late?

The territory in which we now tread in this pilgrimage is where the discovery of hidden gems brings an emphasis to Genesis that is seldom scanned. The chapters under review provide extensive coverage of family, of the familiar, and also foreign alliances. Occasionally an event stands out as holding significant value to the whole. The event that, with good reason, brought about the chastisement of the sons was a result of unmitigated cruelty. The treatment of Shechem (the man), because of his desire for their sister, Dinah, could not be condoned. He was alien to the rigid rules set down for all males of all the descendants of Abraham (chapter 34), and he was unacceptable. The action taken was deplorable!

Jacob then followed the leading of the LORD to return to Bethel. Good move—he was learning to walk in the paths of peace. It was here that *YHVH* reiterated His will that Jacob would undergo the name change: Jacob would indeed become Israel! Chapter 35 announces the death of Isaac and Rachel after Benjamin—*son of my right hand*—had been born. Chapter 36 offers a detailed reporting of the descendants of Esau.

As chapter 37 opens to view, we are confronted with Joseph, and the gem! What a spoiled young lad he proved to be. Be sure to read 37:3–4 for these verses are axiomatic to the whole. But Joseph became proud and pompous. His coat of many colours would have emphasised his pride. Then, the dreams. What did he make of them? His pride earned the rebuke of his dad—a gem? Israel wanted better from his son!

HIDDEN TREASURE: *DELIVERANCE*

The favourite flower will be set above the other garden varieties.

A WORD FROM THE WORD

פליטה

peletah – "deliverance"

The annual Floriade in Canberra is a superb floral tribute to the garden varieties of flowers that flourish in Australia. The view of the central lake allows for a border to display the blooms of spring. Tulips are a choice selection and the beauty of what I saw on that auspicious occasion demanded a photograph that would at least remind me of the splendours all about me on that special occasion. As I turn to the photograph this morning, however, I am drawn to the flower-pot holding those choice blooms. What better "Picture Parable" could there be to express Joseph's, and Israel's, dilemma? There, beside the elevated blooms was a weeping willow. Israel would know his tears!

A VIEWPOINT TO PONDER
How can it be that such beauty could evoke tears?

It is in the loss of great beauty that the deepest grief is known.

Let's face it: young Joseph does not cover himself with glory in the current setting, even though his cloak may be glorious! That cloak, multiplied by the "interpretations" of his dreams, could have led to his early demise. They almost did!

We have already discovered that Israel—his newly re-named father—had most recently administered a rebuke to the young lad. It was so foolish for the boy to be "blooming in the elevated flower-pot" when he was not wholly one of the brothers, nor at one with his brothers, either. Enmity was increasing and Israel feared for his beloved boy—son of Rachel, who was his one true love—as the scriptural records attest so powerfully!

One can just see the boy, grinning his greatness when attempting to lord it over his ten half-brothers. "Look at me: I had a dream last night that told me I was the most important son in this family! You all bowed down to me: I am the best of all the sheaves of wheat!" It should have been enough. Let sleeping dogs lie! But no, there was another dream.

Emboldened by the portent of this further dream, Joseph had the temerity to approach his patient parent to tell, in amazing detail, of how the sun and moon—his parents—and the eleven stars all bowed in reverent homage to the lad! Joseph should have kept his counsel! Where was **deliverance**?

Having been sent out into the fields to take food to his brothers, Joseph was quite unaware of the plots that were aroused by his approach. No doubt he smiled at the ten. No doubt they accepted the victuals! No doubt he would have run from them had he known of their intent. Where is the gem in this less than salubrious account? Where is the good to be found under the surface of such a disturbing state of affairs?

The gem is gleaming in the sunlight! Look to where Reuben stands! When it counted most, Rueben, then Judah stood the test expected of one who would bear the responsibility of leadership. He saved his brother, though into slavery!

HIDDEN TREASURE: *FAVOUR*

The tree that reaches far must be sure that its roots can hold the soil.

A WORD FROM THE WORD

חֵן

chen – "favour"

While travelling with friends, I came upon a quite remarkable tree on the banks of a deep lake situated far to the north of Canada. This was land tempered by fierce winters, the liveliness of spring, the warmth of summer and the grandeur of autumn. Due to its northerly clime, this lake would be frozen when the ice took control, and much mellowed by the warmth that the sun was prone to grant in summer. Though it was already autumn, there was just a hint of it on some external leaves. The truly remarkable aspect of the scene was governed by the strength of the tree that had been pushed out of place by its "siblings", yet able to thrive. Its roots went down deep!

A VIEWPOINT TO PONDER
Can a tree "speak" for humanity's quality of life?

Jesus said, 'Make the tree good and its fruit will also be good. A good man displays goodness from the good stored in him.'

Well, talk about people falling on their feet! Perhaps one of the most outstanding of all such accounts is that of Joseph, willed to die by his brothers, yet saved by Rueben. Judah had also spoken a word on Joseph's behalf (though with monetary motives). The brothers were, therefore, absolved from the taint of murder on their records, though not that of the sin of doing harm to their brother. They could not absolve their souls of guilt. Joseph was sold as a slave and trundled off to Egypt—already commanding an outstanding place in the annals of history. How would the lad Joseph fare in a land so alien to his own?

Joseph has arrived in this foreign country. The language is unknown to him. How will Joseph communicate as required in such an auspicious setting? Joseph has a means beyond the norm and it will become apparent as his service to Potiphar, the Captain of the Palace Guard, developed so astonishingly.

What is it about Joseph that sets him apart from his peers and commends him to the attention of Potiphar? His early life had been less than commendable. And now, with no language skill to support him and lacking in the culture of his captors, Joseph possessed—surprisingly, given his early failures—a sterling character. He lived what he knew to be right with fortitude.

Something of the gracious character of Rachel, his mother, must have rubbed off on him. And there was Jacob, the one-time deceiver who had—by the grace of God—developed a commendable stance because of his walk with the LORD! Yes, Joseph possessed an upright character, the worth of which was noticeable. Joseph had the spiritual stamina to overcome temptation even when "the coast was clear". His confrontation with Potiphar's wife was a pertinent example!

Potiphar had been impressed. The Palace Guard would need to be of highest calibre and this young slave stood head and shoulders above the rest of the staff in terms other than his physique. Joseph earned the **favour**—the gem discovered here—given to him. He was advanced in Court responsibilities.

HIDDEN TREASURE: *KINDNESS*

Why tread through life in shadows when there is sunlight nearby?

A WORD FROM THE WORD

חסד

chesed – "kindness"

It was with some solemnity that I walked along that pathway. The day was sunny, with no breeze though so close to the Southern Ocean. I had just visited the ruins of one of the most notorious penal prisons in Australia's history—Port Arthur! It had been, in a past generation, the dubious "home" of my great grandfather, deported from the U.K. He is listed in the prison's records as having received the "cat-o'-nine-tails" on numerous occasions. The "cat-o'-nine-tails" was a whip of nine leather straps, each entwining jagged iron chips! Life was not good for great grandfather. But, at last, he walked out a free man!

A VIEWPOINT TO PONDER
Can anyone feel truly free again after prison life?

It's not the prison bars, or the fencing, that "bars" one's freedom, it's the bars on the mind and, the heart. Leave the shadows!

PILGRIM'S JOURNAL: Genesis 39 – 40

Joseph is in gaol! A coloured coat, then the subterfuge of a thwarted woman, has placed Joseph in another pit! This time, of the gaol variety! The reader will certainly have to dig deep below the surface of Scripture to find the new gem which, none-the-less, will gleam at its best though housed in the vault of prison. **Kindness**? Where will Joseph find kindness in prison? By being kind. Joseph possessed this gem in large quantities!

Joseph was obviously an outstanding young man. He had arrived in Egypt as an alien slave. He earned the respect of Potiphar—the Captain of the Palace Guard—who would have been more than disappointed when mis-informed of the seeming infidelity. Though free of any culpability, Joseph was cast into prison and, not any ordinary prison, he was incarcerated in the prison attached to the Palace!

How strange! Here was a prisoner caring for other prisoners. Unheard of, indeed! Yet there he was, chatting with prisoners, binding up their wounds, bringing hope where there was no hope! Prisoners found that they could confide in this man. They trusted him. Then, there was that morning when the cup-bearer to the king—that is, Pharoah—told of a strange dream he had experienced. In telling Joseph of his dream, the man was astounded to hear what that dream really meant. He was to be exonerated! He would be freed to serve Pharoah!

The Palace baker, who had listened so intently to the previous interpretation, plucked up courage to tell of his dream. As he related his story, Joseph grew perplexed. The LORD, who was the Source of his interpretations, had made matters clear. The man was guilty and it would be proved so. The baker, in retribution, was to lose his life.

Events turned out as predicted. For one, his sorrow, then oblivion. The other could not contain his joy when it was affirmed that he was free and could resume his employment. He promised to speak up for Joseph. But he forgot! Oh, Joseph!

HIDDEN TREASURE: *REMEMBRANCE*

Famine can drain the soul of life if there is no remembrance of need.

A WORD FROM THE WORD

זכר
zakar – "to remember"

After peering at the map (always a good idea before setting out into unknown territory), it was considered a wise undertaking to choose the route through Death Valley. We were bound for the Grand Canyon—the goal of our latest adventures as tourists. Now, while not having traversed the region prior to this grand foray, we had a more than fair inkling that we would need to go prepared. Plenty of gas in the tank? Yes. Plenty of fluid to slake our thirst? Yes. Plenty of food in the basket? Yes. All ready? Yes. Go for it? Yes. Adequate preparations allowed for trouble-free travel to the magnificent Canyon and beyond!

A VIEWPOINT TO PONDER
Is the goal worth the terrors of such a valley?

One should not attempt death-defying ventures without a certain goal and, have the "food basket" well stocked with faith!

Pharoah was having a hard time of it. He needed his counsellors—the famous soothsayers of Egypt! Of late, his night's slumber had been interspersed with the most confounding dreams. Pharoah tossed and turned. There was no relent. What could the dreams portend? He was the man on whose shoulders, and heart—if he was willing to accept that notion—the blessings and the burdens of Egypt rested. But where was rest? 'Call the magicians! Call the wise men!'

"The Wise" turned up with alacrity. It was worth their lives to do so! Without further ado, Pharoah laid bare the burden of his dreams. What was the import of those two dreams? First, he was pleased with the scene of seven fattened cows feasting on the reeds by the Nile. Suddenly seven famished cows emerged and devoured the healthy beasts. As if that wasn't enough, what next does he see but a second dream where seven ears of grain, grew up from the Nile. Then another reed sprouted, a measly, famished stalk emerged and fed itself on the healthy grain. Pharoah then demanded an immediate interpretation. No one spoke. All were aghast. Nothing came to mind!

It just so happened that a cup-bearer was standing nearby. He was appalled! Yes, *him*! How could he have been so thoughtless as to forget all that Joseph had done for him? Here is the gem: he was now **remembering**. 'Sire, I must own up to my dreadful forgetfulness. While I was in prison awaiting death, there was a Hebrew prisoner, who listened to the dream I had and, also that of the baker. Sire, that Hebrew lad was right. I came back, as he said, to serve you. The baker was hanged.'

'Bring that prisoner to me at once!' Pharoah was intrigued. Joseph was overjoyed to hear the summons. He hastened from the dungeon, washed and shaved, then presented himself to the Pharoah. He listened to the dreams, explained that not he, but the God of Heaven would interpret them: seven years of plenty, seven years of famine in Egypt. The outcome? Joseph became the governor, preparing Egypt for plenty then, famine.

HIDDEN TREASURE: *HONESTY*

Even a desert scene can encourage those who hold to hope.

A WORD FROM THE WORD

כנים
kanim – "honesty"

Central Australia holds many natural wonders. If one is adventurous enough to digress from the main highway, the landscape is pleased to open its treasures of the natural variety. My companions and I were immensely blessed with the sight before us upon reaching the lookout at "The Breakaways": here was "Pepper and Salt", a remarkable outcrop of arid soil yet displaying plainly the reason for the title. So, the condiments were to hand but where was a meal fit to be seasoned with salt (ensure the pure life) and pepper (activate the spiced life)?

A VIEWPOINT TO PONDER
Can a "Picture Parable" deliver the actual requirements?

Parables are used to illustrate a truth. Once a truth is seen, it will be absorbed to the benefit of all. Hold to Truth: it counts!

It was enough to shock any one, let alone Joseph who had said "goodbye" to his earlier life in the land chosen by God for the dynasty of Abraham. Joseph had been "booted" out of his homeland, and his father's tents, by brothers who hated him enough to consider murder. To sell their brother as a slave was tantamount to murder in the mind, anyway!

In considering the saga, however, who can tell if it was not the will of God that this young man was to be the "man of the hour", the man who *YHVH* had prepared to become the Governor of Egypt so that a region-wide famine lasting seven years could be managed. It has already been recognised by readers keen to dig below the surface of the "soil" of Genesis, that here was a man who trusted the LORD to guide and direct his plans to save the land of Egypt. In so doing, look at what happens: here is the "salt and pepper" of the story thus far.

Ten brothers turn up in Egypt—Joseph's brothers. Joseph is courageous enough to remain in control of the situation. He sets a plan in motion that would enable, if at all possible, the reunion of the entire family. Joseph would need to be circumspect.

The negotiations, tenuous as they no doubt were, proved sufficient to determine if there had been any change in the minds of those brothers. They had been so prone to anger and hate that they were prepared to kill. The brothers were now avowing that they were **honest** men. If this can be proven, a true gem has been unearthed!

But what of his own brother, Benjamin? How could Joseph discover the truth of his situation? As an "Egyptian" governor, Joseph could not have known of his existence. And, what of his father, Jacob—Israel? Joseph certainly tied those ten men up in knots! He needed confirmation. The plan he then devised is quite remarkable.

Oh, so they had a younger brother??? Then the "problem" could not be solved until that young man was brought down to Egypt to prove the truth of their avowed honesty.

HIDDEN TREASURE: *SAVIOUR*

When the exit to a tunnel is blocked, one must turn to "*THE RIGHT*"!

A WORD FROM THE WORD

יֹשֵׁעַ

yasha – "saviour"

South Australia is a unique wonder-world! Here we were, travelling through the Eyre Peninsula, when we came upon the "Haystacks"! Stacks they were, but no cattle would ever get their fill by munching on these "haystacks". Moulded in the shape of hay, it is true, but this was nature's trick. These "haystacks" were made of stone! Magnificent, though, in their own way. The desire to wander through nature's tunnel also brought its surprise for yet more haystacks greeted our arrival. How would I find the exit? Look in the right direction!

A VIEWPOINT TO PONDER
How does one negotiate the "tunnels" blocking peace?

What is the source of the blockage? This is a good place to start. What disrupted the peace? Clear that up. You will be free!

Joseph desired to see his father and his only full-blood brother once more. His terms were disastrous. A brother must remain and the youngest son be brought to Egypt to set all things straight. The brothers began to feel the enormity of their prior sins. Reuben then spoke of their penitence. 'We must now give an accounting for what happened!' (chapt. 42:22). The admission of guilt is the gem. And Joseph overheard. In secret, he wept!

The return journey of the sons to Father Jacob—Israel—was grim enough. However, their sombre thoughts took a sudden turn for the worse by the discovery, to their horror, of that money in their sacks! Whoever could have placed it there? For what purpose? They could not have placed it there even by the worst of mistakes in the negotiations! How could they explain the unexplainable to their distraught father? Besides which, they could never return to Egypt for Benjamin would need to accompany them.

The dilemma turned to grief as they arrived home to relate their misfortune—because of the fortune in their sacks! All were resolved never to return to Egypt. Until, that is, because of the extended famine, there was no more fodder for their stock. The family talked through their extremity of need but, in the end, they realised that a return to Egypt was their only means of survival. Judah then offers his very life to be the **saviour** of his brother! At last, Jacob agreed to the need for Benjamin to accompany them though he felt in his heart that the second and last son of Rachel would be lost to him!

That trek to Egypt would have been the most difficult of those brothers' lives. When they fronted up to the Governor, little did they realise what lay ahead. But first, Joseph's "stolen" silver cup! How could they account for it in Benjamin's sack? Benjamin must go to prison but the others were free to return to their home country. Judah spoke up: 'Let me remain, allow Benjamin go home lest his father die of grief. I guaranteed his safety, I promised to bear any blame for him!' Joseph wept!

HIDDEN TREASURE: *"HOME"*

If the Sphinx could speak today, it would remind us of the truly great.

A WORD FROM THE WORD

בית

bayith (beth) – "house" (home)

The southern coastline of Australia is "home" to some spectacular rock formations. "The Twelve Apostles" is the major "must see" of tourists from near and far. They could easily have been named "The Twelve Brothers" for the sons of Jacob have also earned their place in the history of Israel! When visiting the area, my eyes also turned to a lesser known rock-face. I saw a "Sphinx", and as I return to the photo this morning, I see the faces of Israel's "children" nestled beside him. The family are, at last, at home with him. Israel, his boys, stand the test of time.

A VIEWPOINT TO PONDER
How can a "Picture Parable" become truth?

A picture merely evokes a truth, reawakening a memory within, or, it may engender a new thought that holds truth. Think on it.

PILGRIM'S JOURNAL: Genesis 45 – 50

'I am your brother!' Staggered, his kin looked at him in disbelief, then a terror set in. What would Joseph do to repay them for their ill-treatment of him? How would he avenge all the wrongs meted out to him in the past?

Joseph began to weep again. Now, the Egyptian courtiers also heard him. The news was out! 'Come to me, close to me!' and they obeyed. He gave a heartfelt explanation to appease his brothers' fear. 'Do not distress yourselves. It was all for the best! It was the LORD who placed me here. It was to save your lives! It was He who planned for me to become a guardian to Pharoah during this terrible drought. Now I will be able to secure a safe place for you here in Egypt.'

The brothers then felt the warm embrace of Joseph. They were forgiven! All needed to dry their eyes after the reunion. 'Is my father still alive?' Their answer surely warmed his heart. 'You must go to him, tell him all!' Meanwhile, Pharoah had been informed of the reunion of the twelve brothers by the courtiers. He was delighted! He went to them, outlined a magnificent means by which they could return home and bring Israel to Egypt where all their families could live in peace in the choicest area available: Goshen!!!

It is beyond words, let alone "Picture Parables", to tell of Jacob's disbelief, shock, wonder, joy, thankfulness (and all in large measure), at the news. It far outweighed the splendiferous gifts of Pharoah! Immediate plans were made for all the families to relocate, and move down to Egypt. The journey was made by the most lavish means available—made possible by Pharoah! ISRAEL HAD COME "**HOME**"! Home? Egypt was not "The Promised Land"! But tents, and houses, are not homes: the home is where the heart abides—Israel was with his family.

The remaining chapters provide details of family matters. In Israel's blessing to each of his boys, 49:10 rates a mention as it is from this tribe that Jesus is born! Though the book ends "…in a coffin in Egypt", it opens the way to REDEMPTION!

HIDDEN TREASURE: *COMPLETION*

For every colour under the sun there are the colours of the soul.

A WORD FROM THE WORD

כלה
kalah – "finished"

The lad was mesmerised! I had asked him to tell the class what he thought of a slice of sandstone. 'Nothing much. Looks clean enough,' I then asked him to place the stone in a tray of clear water. I am sure he then had trouble keeping his eyes in their sockets! Open-mouthed, amazed, he shouted, 'Look at it. Look at it!' The sandstone—actually, ferruginous sandstone—had been all but transformed into the multifarious colours of an opal!!! The class and I then enjoyed the after-effects of the discovery and all that the colours could say about life and living!

A VIEWPOINT TO PONDER
How is colour found under the earth, away from the sun?

A stone, be it an opal, an emerald or, a ruby, must be true to itself whether in the sun or the dark. Just so, should humankind!

PILGRIM'S JOURNAL: Genesis

The ferruginous aspect of the Coober Pedy (South Australian opal fields), sandstone is of an iron chemical constituent. While not allowing the matrix stone to be discoloured by iron oxide, this chemical is the component that permits the exquisite colouring of the gem to be discernible when placed in water.

As the photo's caption suggests, the colours under the soil can mirror the colours found above the earth! Scan the rainbow and you will be reminded of the colour range God has given us: the red, orange, yellow, green, the blues, and violet. Additions would include the infra-red beyond one end of the spectrum and ultra-violet beyond the other end! This "speaks" of Eternity!

As pilgrims, then, we have been using the proverbial spade to dig below the alluvial soil of Genesis to unearth the deeper treasures ready to share their wealth. It is wise to consider each, and according to the colours we may well affix to them:
There is the red—the "ruby" akin to the blood of sacrifice.
The orange—the "jasper" relative to the warmth of grace.
The yellow—the "topaz" gleaming as does joy.
The green—the "emerald" enlightening the life eternally.
The blue—the "turquoise" of the "primary" quality of purity.
The indigo—the "sapphire" revealing wholeness and holiness.
The violet—the "amethyst": a life surely touched by Royalty.

The spectrum of the "rainbow" colours, found by diligent spade work, has unearthed—via the "**Gems from Genesis**"—the full range of the Biblical story. It is the Gospel story in the first book of the Bible. With the knowledge of the full story, we are able to ascertain the meaning of the Blood of Sacrifice: it is found in the most ancient form of ת as we have discovered: it is the cross: †
There is the warm glow of grace in the story of Cain, of Noah. There is the unbounded joy of the patriarchs, the eternal quality of life as the black in Jacob's life turns to green. There is the pure blue as Abraham decides to walk before the Face of God. It is not too much to ascribe the "sapphire" to Sarah, his wife, who trekked with him through all the years. Joseph is worthy of the robes granted him. The treasury is completed with this gem:

A Gem —Joseph

THE LEADER

My God!
What's this? Do startled eyes
deceive? These men who bow
before me now within the
precincts of my given power.
These men do bear familiar ways!
These Hebrews, shepherds,
yes! I've known them since
my youngest days. How could
I once forget these men?
My brothers: Reuben, Simeon
and Dan! There's present, each
of *ten*? But where's the youngest,
Benjamin? My closest kin,
my mother's younger son.
I love him much for we are two
of one, our father's choicest wife.
Perhaps these men will know regret
when they discover who I am!

My God!
The stars! The "stars" of which
I'd dreamed when in my youth,
and spoke of them in uninvited ways.
My brothers have fulfilled the dream!
They bow in supplication here,
within my own ascended light!
Also, the "sheaves of wheat"
for they are gripped in famine now
and seek my aid! The dreams
of youth do haunt me though, for in
this day, I feel the joy of finding them.
Then, sorrow wraps me in its shroud.

THE LEADER

My father, does he live? And, also,
my Benjamin, what's news of him?
I need to test my brothers now!

O LORD!
How could such brothers change
their heart's desires, their own
most wicked and vindictive ways?
Have they forgotten past misdeeds?
Or, do they mourn for one, long past,
who thoughtless was but meant
no harm? How may I test, detect
an earnest love within them each?
But when my wrath was feigned
to search their truest nature yet,
they fought the while to save the one,
yet not themselves! In this I see
the clearest sign of selflessness:
I surely find their characters
are each refined in truth!

O LORD!
I worship at Your Feet as they
did bow to me in humble gratitude.
I aim to serve You all my days.
My words and deeds will speak
Your praise! For every crisis
and all cares of life I've known,
You meant it for my good, and those
who once had meant me harm.
My heart rejoices in the scene
and I will celebrate once more
the light I saw on father's face,
my brothers' too, for they have found
forgiving grace. I find the family
together, bless'd, and all restored!

THE REFLECTIVE GLANCE

THIS UNORTHODOX APPROACH TO THE STUDY
OF GENESIS HAS OPENED TO VIEW MANY OF THE
HIDDEN TREASURES TO BE FOUND. THE SELECTED
SONG/POEM WILL EMPHASISE ITS WORTH.

* THE PILGRIM'S WAY
Tune: e.g. *Old Hundredth* L.M.

How blessed is the Pilgrim's Way;
We tread the righteous paths of God,
Delighting in His holy Law
And meditating on His word.

How bless'd are those whose chosen path
Is straight and ordered by the LORD!
The boundaries of grace are wide,
Unmeasured as the love of God!

How bless'd are all who trust the LORD,
Our Fortress in all times of need;
He is "The Rock", salvation's guide,
His arms outstretched, our cry to heed.

How bless'd are they who heed His call!
The Path to Life is ever plain;
Abundant is His power to keep:
Our faith in Him need never wane.

Our refuge, our deliverance,
The LORD is sure to walk with us,
Unfailingly His power is shown,
He leads us on in righteousness.

THERE ARE MOUNTAINS AND VALLEYS
TO NEGOTIATE AND WE WILL FIND HIS SHEPHERD
STAFF WILL LEAD US SAFELY HOME.

THE FORWARD GLANCE

GENESIS WILL STAND AS THE PROLOGUE
OF ALL THAT IS TO FOLLOW IN THE BIBLE, FOR EVERY
BOOK THEN RELATES ITS ON-GOING PORTION
OF THE DRAMA OF REDEMPTION.

* ALL TIME IS IN YOUR HANDS
Tune: e.g. *Melita*   8.8.8.8.8.8. Iambic

All time is in Your hands, O LORD:
The past, a heritage of faith,
The present is our "Day of Grace",
The future is unknown to us
But we believe there is a place
For us beyond the days of Earth.

The Earth is in Your hands, O LORD,
This precious world, creation's flower;
And yet we see decay, discord,
In darkest night where sin has soared
And human need sees grief outpoured;
We claim the Saviour's cleansing power.

All things are in Your hands, O LORD!
From the beginning You decreed
That all things work together for
The good if we will love Your Law;
LORD, we will trust You and adore,
For You will walk with us indeed.

Our life is in Your hands, O LORD,
And You have sealed us as Your own;
We trust Your ever precious Name!
From Heaven's Glory once You came
To die for us and take our blame;
You grant Your peace till Heaven's won!

OUR LIVES DO NOT END IN A COFFIN IN EGYPT,
OUR LIVES ARE MEANT FOR ETERNAL GLORY!

THE HEBREW ALPHABET

MODERN FORM: **ANCIENT FORM:**

Modern	Name	Ancient	Meaning
א	aleph	OX:	Supreme, Able
ב	beth	HOUSE:	Home, Abiding
ג	gimel	CAMEL:	Enduring, Dependable
ד	daleth	DOOR:	Entrance, Access
ה	he	WINDOW:	Looking, Revealing
ו	vav	HOOK:	Connecting, Holding
ז	zain	SEED:	Life, Heritage
ח	<u>ch</u>eth	FENCE:	Fellowship, Company
ט	teth	SNAKE:	Opposition, Danger
י	yod	HAND:	Work, Worship
ך כ	kaph	" OPENED:	Labour, Kindness
ל	lamed	STAFF:	Teaching, Learning
ם מ	mem	SEA:	Chaos, Peace
ן נ	nun	FISH:	Strength, Persistence
ס	same<u>ch</u>	CHARIOT:	Support, Uphold
ע	ain	EYES:	Vision, Watching
ף פ	pe	MOUTH:	Face, Witnessing
ץ צ	tzaddi	MOTHER	WITH BABY: Nurture
ק	qoph	WEAPON:	Control, Power
ר	resh	HEAD:	Leadership, Wisdom
ש	sin/shin	TEETH:	Guard, Crush
ת	tav: †	CROSS:	A Sign, Salvation

The "Picture Parables" in Hebrew can convey ideas (eg: "sea" never rough at end of word—see מ ם). The ancient form of letters can add much to a story!

158

A SONG/POEM FOR CONTEMPLATION

By going in search of what the ancient world has to offer a pilgrim, it is opportune to focus on the language of The Book long before the coming of Jesus. Hebrew is here presented in a poem in the form of the Psalms that follow the acrostic mode: The words in bold represent the meaning in the ancient letters.

AN *alephbeth* PSALM
(Acrostic – a mode of Hebrew Poetry)

for

YESTERDAY	TODAY	TOMORROW
Confirmation	Thanksgiving	Hopefulness

א *aleph*   First and **foremost**, You are *Elohim*, Eternal God;
I honour and adore Your Holy Name.

ב *beth*   LORD, You are my Refuge and my Sanctuary.
I find my one true **home** in You.

ג *gimel*   You lead me on the mountains, in deep valleys
and in arid desert lands; I do not fear my **pilgrimage**.

ד *daleth*   The **door** You open, *YHVH*, leads to abundant life;
in going out I find my joy and, coming in, my rest.

ה *he*   Your **windows** open out to vistas glorious;
Your wondrous grace is always in my view.

ו *vav*   O LORD, I am secure when **held** by You;
Your loving-kindness never fails; I will not fall.

ז *zain*   In You is **Life**; O *Elohim*, You give me strength;
I grow in knowledge of Your will from day to day.

An *alephbeth* Psalm

ח   *cheth*   LORD, You "**companion**" me, I find You near;
          You walk with me, reveal my way through life.

ט   *teth*   When **evil** threatens, I will look to You for help;
          in goodness and in kindness You will tend my soul.

י   *yod*   I hold Your **hand**, I am secure: You care for me;
          I am Your child, You reach right down to me.

כ   *kaph*   In Your **open hand** is all I need;
          in body, mind, and soul I am replete.

ל   *lamed*   You have **instructed** me in all the way that I should go;
          Your discipline encourages me to be upright.

מ   *mem*   You are the LORD of turbulent and troubled **seas**;
          when I am terrified, You calm the storm for me.

נ   *nun*   You **challenge** me to face my fears;
          I'll take the route You mark for me.

ס   *samekh*   O LORD, You will **support** and strengthen me;
          rough country is made smooth by Your own help.

ע   *ayin*   My **eyes** are focused on the LORD
          and where You lead, I follow on.

פ   *pe*   I am to walk before the **Face** of *Elohim*;
          it is the LORD who makes me whole.

צ   *tsaddi*   From before my birth, O LORD, You have **nurtured** me;
          as I follow Your decrees, my life will be enhanced.

An *alephbeth* Psalm

ק   *qoph*   All Your commands are **sure**, there is no uncertainty!

You issue Your decrees with powerful emphasis.

ר   *resh*   My **mind** is stayed on *Elohim*, my God;

You do instruct me how to choose the right.

ש   *shin*   The LORD my Shield, Refuge; You are my **guard**;

My safety is assured as I rely on You to guide.

ת   *Tav:* †   I know my great **Redeemer**: You have set me free;

You offer me Your life that I may have true life!

www.ingramcontent.com/pod-product-compliance
Lightning Source LLC
Chambersburg PA
CBHW040844120626
46547CB00001B/24